Guide to
The Great Attractions of
Los Angeles and Beyond

Guide to
The Great Attractions of Los Angeles and Beyond

by
Frederick J. Pratson

A Voyager Book

The Globe Pequot Press

Chester, Connecticut

─DISCLAIMER─

Although the author has received and used information and photographs from many different sources, *this guide is not an official publication of any company, association, or government agency mentioned or described herein.* This guide has been independently researched and written by the author and independently produced and marketed by the publisher. Within this guide, reference is made to a number of attractions, rides, systems, components, entities, products, fictional and animal characters, processes, and the like that are protected by copyrights and trademarks, both registered and pending, used by particular companies, attractions, and entertainments that own them. No attempt has been made by the author and the publisher of this guide to infringe these and other copyrights and trademarks. Every effort has been made to present this trademarked and copyrighted material in those contexts to which they legally and properly belong and to no other.

Every effort has been made so that the material contained in this guide is current and accurate. The author and the publisher are responsible neither for inadvertent errors or material that becomes obsolete due to circumstances beyond their control nor for changes made by others that are either unknown or not communicated to the author and publisher before publication.

Library of Congress Cataloging-in-Publication Data

Pratson, Frederick John.
  Guide to the great attractions of Los Angeles and beyond / by Frederick Pratson. — 1st ed.
    p. cm.
  Includes index.
  ISBN 0-87106-537-1
  1. Los Angeles (Calif.)—Description—Guide-books. 2. Los Angeles Region (Calif.)—Description and travel—Guide-books. 3. Hollywood (Los Angeles, Calif.)—Description—Guide-books. I. Title.
F869.L83P73 1989
917.94'940453—dc20   89-34760
                                                                   CIP

Manufactured in the United States of America
First Edition/First Printing

**For my children
and their California dreams.**

About the Author

Frederick Pratson is author of several books, among them *Guide to the Great Attractions of Orlando and Beyond, Guide to Washington, D.C. and Beyond, Guide to Cape Cod, Guide to Eastern Canada, Guide to Western Canada,* and *Consumer's Guide to Package Travel around the World.*

Mr. Pratson has also published articles in *The Boston Globe, Christian Science Monitor, Smithsonian, Yankee,* and other magazines and newspapers. He is a member of the Society of American Travel Writers.

Contents

Southern California: A Personal View

I first traveled to Los Angeles in the early 1970s and, coming from starchy New England, experienced a culture shock of considerable proportion—but, to my delight, a pleasant one. Except for driving the infamous freeways, which frightened the Boston baked beans out of me (they no longer do, except at morning and evening rush hours), it didn't take me long at all to become immersed in an immensely attractive and comfortable style of living that has served to make California the most populous and one of the most dynamic states in America.

It is said that our nineteenth-century American concept of Manifest Destiny was to create one nation from the Atlantic to the Pacific. This was so, and thus California became part of the Union. The lure of eternally sunny beaches with bikini-clad maidens and muscled surfers, ripened avocados stuffed with abalone for lunch, and "gold in them thar hills" (not so much real gold but real estate and hot movie deals) have been among the many forces driving countless persons to come here seeking their own personal manifest destiny.

I must admit that I am one of these seekers at heart and in spirit, but my body continues to reside in Calvinist New England. Why continue on? I ask, in a plaintive voice, when all of me could be strolling the golden beach at Malibu, Santa Barbara, La Jolla, or Coronado . . . or roller-skating on the asphalt paths of Venice Beach with all the other joyous cuckoos . . . or making mega-money deals in the hills of Bel Air . . . or chasing a pockmarked little white ball on the ever-lush links at Rancho Mirage. I have a date with my shrink to

A PERSONAL VIEW

delve into what is keeping me from becoming California bound, not just for another visit but permanently. California is that powerful a seductress. Enchanting, wacky, exciting, gorgeous Southern California, even with its many outrageous imperfections, is, I have found, a lusty place, and so should it be enjoyed. I envy you who are on your way there ahead of me.

1

Introduction to Greater Los Angeles and Beyond

Greater Los Angeles, including Orange County, is like an amoeba of people and their habitations irrepressibly spreading out over the broad flatlands and valleys between the Pacific Ocean and the San Gabriel, Santa Monica, and San Bernardino mountain ranges. This huge metropolitan sprawl is an area of many communities, including the city of Los Angeles, Hollywood, Beverly Hills, Bel Air, Westwood, Burbank, Malibu, Santa Monica, Venice, Marina del Rey, Century City, Torrance, Pasadena, Long Beach, Anaheim, and Garden Grove. Los Angeles is California's largest (and the nation's second-largest) city. Here, within the metropolitan area, live more than thirteen million people of every race and ethnicity.

Thousands of new people move into Los Angeles every week, a great many to stay permanently. They come from other parts of the country and from other nations, attracted by the ideal climate, enticing life-style, and progressive economy. Others come as refugees, fleeing brutal regimes, and illegally from Mexico and other Latin American countries. Spanish is Southern California's second language, after English; in some areas it is the first and only language.

This strong Spanish influence must seem foreign to many visitors, but it should not. The Los Angeles coast was first visited by the Portuguese explorer Juan Rodriguez Cabrilho (a name you will find in many places throughout Southern California) in 1542. Los Angeles itself was founded by Franciscan priests as a mission for Yangna

3

INTRODUCTION

Indians in 1771. This was one in a chain of twenty-one missions established in Alta ("high") California. In 1781, on present Olvera Street in the heart of downtown Los Angeles, eleven families from Mexico dedicated their new community to the Virgin Mary and named their pueblo El Pueblo del la Reina de Los Angeles, or the City of the Angels.

In the 1800s Mexico separated itself from Spain, and California became part of that new nation's territory. Through its Spanish/Mexican periods, Los Angeles was a ranching economy based on cattle and horses. After the Mexican War (1846–47), Alta California was ceded to the United States by the Treaty of Guadalupe Hidalgo in 1848; Baja (lower) California was retained by Mexico. Yankee settlers and entrepreneurs came in like a swarm of locusts, and the transformation of Los Angeles began. Oil was discovered. Real estate boomed. New industries were established. Hollywood became "Tinsel Town." Greater Los Angeles continues to change and grow, but a Spanish/Latin American ambience persists, softening hard edges and making many aspects of the city lovely and lyrical.

Although visitors tend to think of Greater Los Angeles in terms of the entertainment business—movies, television, records, and so forth—the economy is far broader. Aerospace, computers, tourism, finance, agriculture, petroleum production and refining, retailing, education, medicine, and other industries are among the area's main employers. In addition, Greater Los Angeles benefits, through trade and other exchanges, from the now-prosperous or soon-to-be-so nations of the Pacific Rim—Japan, Hong Kong, Taiwan, the People's Republic of China, Korea, and so on—whose economies are burgeoning. Right now the biggest-spending tourists are the Japanese. The City of Los Angeles and other large communities in Southern California have their Chinatowns, Little Tokyos, Little Koreas, and other dynamic ethnic enclaves.

The **Greater Los Angeles Visitor and Convention Bureau** has divided this huge area into five tourist regions (free maps showing and describing these regions are provided by the bureau). The Downtown Los Angeles Region contains Chinatown, Dodger Stadium, Exposition Park (the Afro-American Museum, the Natural History Museum, the Museum of Science and Industry, and the University of Southern California), the Children's Museum, Theatre Center, the Music Centre, Olvera Street/El Pueblo de Los Angeles Historic Park, the Financial District, the Museum of Contemporary Art, the Garment District, the Pacific Stock Exchange, the Jewelry District, and Los Angeles Convention Center.

4

INTRODUCTION

The Westside Region contains Beverly Hills, Century City, the Mormon Temple Visitor Center, the Rodeo Drive shopping area, the ABC Entertainment Center, the University of California at Los Angeles (UCLA), and Westwood Village.

The Hollywood Region has the Universal Studios Tour, the NBC Studio Tour, ABC TV Studios, Burbank Studios, Capitol Records, CBS TV Studios, Farmers Market and Shopping Village, the Gene Autry Western Heritage Museum, Griffith Park, La Brea Tar Pits, the Hollywood Bowl, the Hollywood Studio Museum, the Hollywood Wax Museum, and the Los Angeles County Museum of Art. Here also are Mann's Chinese Theatre, the Max Factor Museum, and the Walk of Fame.

The Coastal Region encompasses Alpine Village in Torrance, the Cabrillo Marine Museum in San Pedro, Culver City, the Forum in Inglewood, Fisherman's Village in Marina del Rey, Hermosa Beach, the Hollywood Race Track, the J. Paul Getty Museum in Malibu, Los Angeles International Airport, Malibu, Manhattan Beach, Marina del Rey, Catalina Island reached from Long Beach and San Pedro, Playa del Rey, Ports O'Call in San Pedro, the *Queen Mary* and the *Spruce Goose* in Long Beach, Santa Monica, the South Coast Botanical Gardens and the Wayfarers Chapel in Palos Verdes, Venice Beach, and Will Rogers State Historic Park in Pacific Palisades.

The San Fernando and San Gabriel Valleys Region has the Rose Bowl, the Ambassador Auditorium, California Institute of Technology, the Norton Simon Museum of Art, and the Pacific Asia Museum, all in Pasadena; the Descanso Gardens in La Canada; and Forest Lawn Memorial Park in Glendale. This region also contains the Huntington Library, Art Gallery, and Botanical Gardens in San Marino, Los Angeles State and County Arboretum and Santa Anita Park in Arcadia, Mission San Fernando in San Fernando, Mission San Gabriel in San Gabriel, and Six Flags Magic Mountain in Valencia.

Orange County, located just to the south and southeast of Los Angeles County, is highly conservative politically. This is in contrast to liberal Santa Monica in Los Angeles County, sometimes called the People's Republic of Santa Monica because of the views of such controversial residents as Jane Fonda. Within Orange County are the city of Anaheim and Buena Park, where you will find Disneyland and Knott's Berry Farm, respectively. Also in Buena Park are Medieval Times and the Movieland Wax Museum, and in Garden Grove is the Crystal Cathedral. Other Orange County attractions include Los Alamitos Race Course, the South Coast Shopping Plaza in Costa

5

INTRODUCTION

Mesa, and the Peters Landing shopping and dining complex in Huntington Beach.

In addition to covering Hollywood and the Greater Los Angeles area, this guide also includes Santa Barbara, a small, flowerlike city located only 90 miles to the northwest of Los Angeles; the Greater Palm Springs area, a splendid resort oasis and world golfing mecca located about 100 miles to the southeast of Los Angeles; and the Greater San Diego area, one of America's favorite, friendliest cities, located 120 miles south of Los Angeles.

If you have never visited Southern California, make a list of the places you "must see" and the things you "must do," such as taking the Universal Studios Tour, visiting Disneyland, and touring Hollywood and Beverly Hills. Just taking in the major attractions and touring around will easily consume a great deal of your vacation time. Be sure, however, to leave some time for relaxing. There is so much to do and see in Southern California that it is easy to poop out and go home exhausted. Loaf at the beaches and be pampered at the resorts. Take some of the laid-back life-style home with you. Memories of such pleasures will linger when "el cheapo" souvenirs have long been junked.

If you have already seen Disneyland and the other biggies, your next visit might be devoted to special experiences, such as going up the coast to lovely Santa Barbara, spending a couple of days golfing or receiving a health and fitness treatment at a deluxe resort in Palm Springs, seeing famous fine art at the Getty Museum, going window shopping along ultraexpensive Rodeo Drive or browsing through the chic stores at South Coast Shopping Plaza, being part of the strange crowd at Venice Beach (everybody is strange here, even those who do not think they are), or taking in the grand and glorious sights of San Diego, with a side trip to nearby Baja Mexico for exciting bullfights and great shopping bargains.

To be honest, you will never have enough time to spend in Los Angeles and all the other wonderful places in Southern California; it will all go by too quickly. But you can always come back for more.

2

Travel Information

This guide is organized to help you in two important ways: (a) as a reference for planning your trip before you leave home and (b) as a source of information and suggestions while traveling.

If you are using this guide for pretrip planning, create a preliminary itinerary. On a sheet of paper, write down the actual days you will be spending in Los Angeles and Southern California, and under each day list the hotel in which you want to stay, the attractions you want to visit, the restaurants at which you want to dine, and the entertainment, shopping, and recreational activities you want to do. This guide contains information in all these essential categories.

Some people religiously follow their itineraries from A to Z, without the slightest deviation. Others start making changes from the moment they arrive at their destination. Many travelers operate between these two extremes. The itinerary sees us through the trip, but there is always something new that catches our fancy and makes for a change. The many attractions listed in this guide give you a wide variety of interesting choices when you get to Los Angeles and tour Southern California. The planning process, before and during the trip, is for many of us part of the fun and challenge of travel.

If you wish to be relieved of decision making about the trip, take a comprehensive package vacation in which just about every detail (air and land transportation, hotels, meals, sightseeing, attractions, entertainment, tips, baggage handling, etc.) is handled by a reputable tour operator. Your hometown travel agent can help you select and book the best vacation package at the right price for when you want to go. Maupintour of Lawrence, Kansas (913–843–1211), is one of the best tour operators in the business. There are many others.

TRAVEL INFORMATION

If you want to make reservations on your own or need more information on a particular accommodation, restaurant, or attraction, this guide provides telephone numbers, including toll-free numbers for many hotels. It is recommended that you make reservations for places of accommodation (hotels, resorts, motels, B&Bs, inns, campgrounds) before you leave home. Your hometown travel agent will, without charge, book rooms for you at leading hotels, resorts, and inns. If you make a change in your itinerary, such as taking a side trip to Palm Springs before heading to San Diego, this guide suggests where to stay, how to get there, and what to do. Information on when attractions are open and at what times is also provided. Operating schedules, however, are subject to change without notice; be sure either to call ahead or to verify schedules through your hotel's concierge or guest relations person.

Although this guide contains a few simple maps to help orient you, you will want to obtain more detailed ones for touring Southern California and for pinpointing the places you want to visit. Free maps are available from the tourist bureaus listed in this guide and from your auto and travel clubs. Sometimes travel agents provide free maps to popular destinations like Los Angeles and Southern California. Low-cost maps and atlases, such as those published by Rand MacNally, are available in bookshops and other kinds of stores. While you are on the road, you can also buy maps at many Southern California gas stations and convenience stores.

Calculating Costs

The cost of accommodations in Southern California varies according to season, location, and level of visitor activity. For example, the cost of a hotel room in Los Angeles tends to be higher during official vacation periods or when large conventions are in the area. The law of supply and demand is at work: the more people wanting rooms, the maximum the price charged; the fewer people needing rooms, the greater the opportunity for lower rates. During times of low activity, many places advertise special bargain rates in newspaper travel sections or provide this information to travel agents, such as those in your hometown. Another example is the resorts of the Greater Palm Springs area, which adjust their rates according to season: the highest rates during the mild-weather winter months and the lowest rates during the hot summer period.

This guide does not use actual dollar amounts, because changes in prices are as predictable as California's sunshine. Accommodations listed herein are, however, designated by price category: **inexpensive** = up to $50 a night for a single or double room; **moderate** = $50 to $100; **expensive** = more than $100 a night. Dining is similarly designated: **inexpensive** = under $25 for two adults having lunch or dinner; **moderate** = up to $60; **expensive** = more than $60. Attractions are designated **admission charge, free,** or **donation.**

You can save money on accommodations by purchasing special package plans, which many hotels offer for weekends, for families, and for a variety of other circumstances. Ask about children's rates or arrangements whereby children, up to a certain age, stay free with parents; ask also about lower rates for senior citizens or government employees and special corporate, auto or travel club, professional association, or fraternal club rates. Ask your hometown travel agent to help you use whatever leverage you can to lower the cost of accommodations, an expensive item in your travel budget.

If you are traveling by plane, watch the travel section of your newspaper for bargains; prices go up and down like an escalator. APEX (advance purchase) fares are among the lowest, but they carry cash penalties if you cancel or make last-minute changes. Again, your hometown travel agent should be contacted for some of the best deals.

The cost of meals in Los Angeles and the rest of Southern California is about the same as where you live, that is, if you live in the United States. If you are coming from Europe or Japan, just about everything (the best in accommodations and dining) will seem inexpensive in comparison to what you pay at home, because of the lower value of the American dollar vis-à-vis the yen, pound, mark, or Swiss franc. If you are coming from Canada, you already know that the California sunshine will cost a tad extra—up to 30 percent, the difference between Canadian and American dollars.

Attractions in Southern California are reasonably priced. Many have lower prices for children up to a certain age, senior citizens, persons traveling with groups, military persons, and others. All the mega-attractions in Southern California—Disneyland, Sea World, Knott's Berry Farm, the Universal City Tour, and so on—are costly, especially for a family of several persons, but offer so much entertainment value and fun in such wholesome environments that few visitors resist paying the admission.

Tipping in Southern California is the same as elsewhere: 15 percent of the bill, excluding tax, for restaurant waiters, as well as for wine stewards in better restaurants, and 20 percent if the service is exceptional; 50 cents to $1 per bag for bellhops, door attendants, and skycaps; $2 to $5 a night for room attendants in hotels and resorts; $1 to $2 for valet-parking attendants; and 15 to 20 percent of the fare for taxi drivers.

How to Get to Los Angeles

Greater Los Angeles and Southern California are major world destinations. Interstate highways lead to Los Angeles from every region in the United States and from Canada. Several airports serve Los Angeles, with Los Angeles International, also called LAX, being the largest. Los Angeles is an important seaport, and various cruise lines depart from here to vacation destinations in Mexico, South America, western Canada, Alaska, and the countries of the Pacific Rim. Los Angeles is also served by regularly scheduled train and bus service.

BY CAR

The following U.S. interstate highways converge on Los Angeles: Interstate 5 from San Francisco, Oregon, Washington, and British Columbia (Canada) to the north and from San Diego and Baja Mexico to the south; Interstate 10 from Palm Springs, Phoenix, Tucson, El Paso, San Antonio, Houston, New Orleans, and Jacksonville (Florida) to the east; Interstate 40 from Albuquerque, Oklahoma City, Little Rock, Memphis, Nashville, and Winston-Salem (North Carolina) to the east; and Interstate 15 from Las Vegas, Salt Lake City, Great Falls (Montana), and Alberta (Canada) to the northeast. Scenic Highway 1, also known as the Pacific Coast Highway, runs almost the entire length of California and is closest to beaches and ocean.

BY AIR

Greater Los Angeles is served by several airports: Los Angeles International (LAX) in Inglewood, Long Beach Airport, John Wayne Airport, Burbank-Glendale Airport, Van Nuys Airport, and Ontario Airport.

TRAVEL INFORMATION

The majority of travelers arrive at and depart from LAX, located 16 miles to the southwest of downtown Los Angeles; the airport information number is (213) 646–5252. Close to seventy international, national, and regional air carriers, such as USAir and British Air, serve LAX.

LAX is one of the busiest airports in the world, but the handling of passengers in the several terminals is efficient and not too confusing for first-time visitors. The modern terminals have comfortable seating areas, private airline clubs, restaurants, lounges, shops, and many other passenger amenities. Special free shuttle buses take travelers making connections between terminals; these shuttles are painted white with blue and green stripes and are marked "LAX Shuttle." There are many parking lots and garages within and outside the airport complex. Nearby hotels provide courtesy transportation to and from LAX.

Airport transportation is provided throughout the Greater Los Angeles area for a reasonable fee by Prime Time Shuttle, Super Shuttle, and other companies. In the baggage collection area are an information board that lists the various ground-transportation options and free telephones for making contact with them. In addition, outside the terminals, as you leave the baggage area, are ground-transportation information booths that will direct you to services (shuttles, buses, taxis, etc.) which will take you where you want to go. Taxis and limousines are also available at the airport but cost more than other available forms of ground transportation. Public bus service (Southern California Rapid Transit District, or RTD) can take you throughout the metropolitan area, but this option is not recommended for those unfamiliar with Los Angeles; otherwise, it is an inexpensive way to get around.

Several of the major auto-rental companies have booths at the terminals or offices near them (contacted by phone and reached via free shuttle). It is recommended that you make a confirmed reservation for a rental car *before* you arrive at LAX, both for certain availability and for the best price.

If you are driving a rental car to downtown Los Angeles from LAX, take the San Diego Freeway (Interstate 405) north to the Santa Monica Freeway (Interstate 10) east. The worst-possible times to drive the freeways from or to the airport are during morning and evening commuter rush hours, from 7:00 to 10:00 A.M. and from 3:30 to 6:00 P.M. If you are new to the roads, use other forms of ground transportation. An alternative way to drive downtown from the airport while avoiding the freeways is to take Lincoln Boulevard North to Wilshire Boulevard East. Wilshire ends right in the heart of down-town.

If you want to get to the Disneyland area from LAX, take the San Diego Freeway (Interstate 405) south to the Garden Grove Freeway (Highway 22) east to the Santa Ana Freeway (Interstate 5) north; take the Stanton Avenue or Ball Road exits off the Santa Ana Freeway. It is recommended that you make use of available ground transpor-tation to Disneyland area hotels. You can then pick up your rental car at or near your hotel.

BY TRAIN

Daily, regularly scheduled rail service is available to Los An-geles and other West Coast cities from various parts of the United States and from Canada through Via Rail and Amtrak connections. Union Station, a lovely historic building in Los Angeles, is located downtown on Alameda Street, across from El Pueblo de Los Angeles Historic District. For fare and schedule information, call Amtrak at (800) 872–7245.

BY BUS

Greyhound provides daily, regularly scheduled bus service to Los Angeles from major cities throughout the United States and Canada. The bus terminal is located on San Pedro Street, between Sixth and Seventh streets. For more information on fares and sched-ules, call (213) 620–1200.

How to Get around Los Angeles

A vehicle, your own or a rented one, is necessary for getting around this huge area and to attractions.

Although Greater Los Angeles sprawls over the landscape seemingly incomprehensively, it is not difficult to get around while driving your own or a rental vehicle. If you are a first-time driver in Los Angeles, do obtain a detailed city map (available at bookshops or from car-rental agencies) and study the layout of the freeways and the main streets and where the attractions you want to visit are located. Many Los Angeles attractions are relatively close to one another. Orange Country attractions, Disneyland, Knott's Berry Farm, and so on, are about a thirty-minute drive on the freeways from downtown Los Angeles.

Orange County has over forty miles of inviting coastline.

TRAVEL INFORMATION

BY CAR

The major Los Angeles freeways are the Santa Monica Freeway (Interstate 10), which goes from Santa Monica on the coast inland to downtown Los Angeles; the San Diego Freeway (Interstate 405), which goes from the Westwood, Bel Air, and Beverly Hills areas past LAX to Long Beach and Orange County; the Hollywood Freeway (Highway 101), which goes from downtown Los Angeles to Hollywood and Universal Studios; and the Santa Ana Freeway (Interstate 5), which goes from Burbank through downtown Los Angeles to Anaheim and is the best access to Disneyland. Try to avoid driving the freeways during commuter rush hours—mornings 7:00 to 10:00 A.M. and evenings from 3:30 to 6:00 P.M.

Horror stories abound about lunatic drivers on the freeways taking gunshots at other drivers or wheeling their cars in and out of lanes like dervishes. Some of these reports are true, particularly when irresponsible or mentally disturbed persons get impatient in heavy traffic. The chance of running into this kind of trouble is, however, remote. My own driving experience in Los Angeles has been without incident; indeed, I found the drivers to be safety conscious and courteous. Still, there are crazies and drunk drivers on every road in America.

There are other key roads in Los Angeles that provide access to many of the area's attractions. One of the most important is Wilshire Boulevard, which runs from the heart of downtown Los Angeles west to the Pacific Coast Highway and the beach in Santa Monica. Along or off Wilshire you will find various museums; deluxe hotels; top restaurants; access to Hollywood, Griffith Park, Beverly Hills, Rodeo Drive, Westwood, and the campus of UCLA; major shopping centers; and the beaches of Santa Monica, Malibu, Venice, and others along the coast.

Sunset and Hollywood boulevards also run east-west and go through Hollywood and the fashionable areas of West Hollywood, Beverly Hills, and Westwood; exclusive Bel Air is west of Beverly Hills and off Sunset Boulevard. Venice Boulevard, running east-west, gives access to Culver City, Venice Beach, and Marina del Rey. The Pacific Coast Highway (north-south Highway 1) provides access to all the coastal communities and their beaches in Greater Los Angeles and Orange County, from Malibu to Laguna.

The main streets and areas in downtown Los Angeles are the Financial District, between east-west Wilshire Boulevard to Second Street, and between north-south Figueroa Street and Grand Avenue; the Jewelry District, between north-south Olive and Hill streets and between east-west Sixth and Twelfth streets; the Garment District, between north-south Main and San Pedro streets and between east-west Seventh and Eleventh streets; Little Tokyo, between north-south San Pedro Street and Central Avenue and between east-west Beverly Boulevard and Third Street; and El Pueblo de Los Angeles Historic District (Olvera Street area), between north-south Main and Alameda streets and the Santa Ana Freeway to the south.

Also within downtown Los Angeles you will find Pershing Park, the Pacific Stock Exchange, the World Trade Center, the Crocker Center, California Plaza, Bonaventure Shopping Gallery, the ARCO Plaza, Los Angeles Theatre Centre, Los Angeles Convention Center, the Music Center, City Hall, Chinatown, the Variety Arts Center, Grand Central Market, Los Angeles Public Library, Dodger Stadium, Olvera Street, and many other points of interest.

RENTAL CARS

All the large national rental-car companies and a number of local ones have facilities at LAX, in downtown Los Angeles, and at other locations in the metropolitan region. Reserve a rental car and get the best deal before you leave home. Use any discounts you might have, such as those offered by the American Association of Retired Persons (AARP) and business, fraternal, and professional organizations to which you belong. If renting from within Los Angeles, shop around by phone or with the help of your hotel's concierge or guest relations person to get the best price. You must be over twenty-one to rent a car and must have a valid driver's license. Major credit cards or a hefty cash deposit is also required for rentals.

BY PUBLIC TRANSPORTATION

Public transportation has long been neglected in Los Angeles in favor of private autos and freeways. Because the city and its satellites are frequently clogged with traffic, Los Angeles is seeking mass-transportation remedies. At present the city is constructing a new subway system that will extend from downtown to major centers in the area. This rapid transit system will not be available for the public until the early to mid-1990s.

The DASH Shuttle provides low-cost public transportation to principal downtown–Los Angeles business, government, retail, and entertainment areas. The DASH Shuttle schedule is as follows: 7:00 to 11:00 A.M., every ten minutes; 11:00 A.M. to 2:00 P.M., every six minutes; 2:00 to 6:00 P.M., every eight minutes; Saturday, 10:00 A.M. to 5:00 P.M., every fifteen minutes; and no service on Sunday and legal holidays. For more information while in Los Angeles, call (800) 8–SHUTTLE.

RTD buses provide service throughout Greater Los Angeles and Orange County at low cost. The use of this service is not recommended unless you have some familiarity with the city and how the buses operate. Drivers do not make change, and exact fare is required. At this writing, the basic fare is $1.10, plus 25 cents for transfers. For current fare and routing information, call RTD's downtown number, (213) 626–4455.

TAXIS AND LIMOUSINES

Taxis are readily available throughout Greater Los Angeles but do not cruise around looking for customers. The best place to get a taxi is in front of a hotel, or you can order one yourself from the following companies:

Los Angeles Taxi, (213) 627–7000
Independent Cab Company, (213) 385–8294
United Independent Taxi, (213) 653–5050

Many of the better hotels offer free or low-cost limousine or shuttle service to airports.

For those in the chips who want to ride in style, the following limousine companies are recommended:

Barrons Limousine Service, (213) 643–6002
Dunhill Limousine Service, (213) 770–4383
Sedan by Michael's, Inc., (818) 763–1190
Dave El Limousines, (213) 550–0070 or (800) 328–3526

Guided Tours of Hollywood and Los Angeles

One of the best ways of getting oriented to a new city, especially one as vast as Los Angeles, is to take guided tours at the beginning of your visit. Tours will dispel some of the confusion and make you more confident to take on the rest of the touring on your own. In addition, guided tours are perfect for those who would rather have others do the driving and provide commentary on the sights.

TRAVEL INFORMATION

Following are a few of the many companies in the area that provide regularly scheduled guided tours of Hollywood and other Greater Los Angeles attractions (have your hotel concierge or guest relations person make tour arrangements for you; some tour companies make pickups at hotels):

Casablanca Tours, (213) 461–0156—homes of the stars, Universal City, Disneyland, and other attractions
Blue Line Tour, (213) 312–3326—the Getty Museum and coastal beaches
Gray Line Tours, (213) 481–2121—a wide variety of tours of Hollywood, Los Angeles, and Southern California
Hollywood Fantasy Tours, (213) 469–8184—tours of Hollywood, Universal City, and nightlife
Oskar J. Tours, (818) 785–4039—city tours and visits to Disneyland, Universal Studios, and other attractions
Tiffany Tours, (213) 642–0555—several different tours of the Los Angeles area, main attractions, and Hollywood

WALKING TOURS
Maps for walking tours are available at the Visitor Information Center, 695 South Figueroa Street; (213) 689-8822. Maps and other touring information are usually available at hotels and other places of accommodation.

Los Angeles Area Tourism Information (see also chapters 9 and 10)

Greater Los Angeles Visitor and Convention Bureau
Downtown Visitor Information Center
695 South Figueroa Street
(213) 689–8822
Open 8:00 A.M. to 5:00 P.M. Monday through Friday

Hollywood Visitor Information Center
The Janes House, Janes House Square
6541 Hollywood Boulevard
(213) 461–4213
Open 9:00 A.M. to 5:00 P.M. Monday through Friday

The Greater Los Angeles Visitor and Convention Bureau publishes *Datelines,* a quarterly calendar of special programs and events that is available at the visitor information centers or through the mail. The bureau also offers *Artsline,* a bimonthly guide on current visual and performing arts events in and around Greater Los Angeles. For copies, write GLAVCB, 695 South Figueroa Street, Los Angeles, California 90071, or call (213) 689–8822.

Other area visitor and convention bureaus to contact:

Anaheim Area Visitor and Convention Bureau
800 West Katella Avenue
P.O. Box 4270
Anaheim 92803
(714) 999–8941

Pasadena Convention and Visitors Bureau
171 South Los Robles Avenue
Pasadena 91011
(818) 795–9311

Long Beach Area Convention and Visitors Council
180 East Ocean Boulevard
Suite 150, Plaza Level
Long Beach 90802
(213) 436–3645

Publications

For up-to-date information on what is happening in Greater Los Angeles while you are visiting, look into the following publications: *Los Angeles Magazine* (monthly, at newsstands), *The Los Angeles Times* and *The Los Angeles Herald Examiner* (daily, at newsstands), *L.A. Weekly* (free), *Key* (free, in hotels), and *Where* (free, in hotels). Many hotels also broadcast current events information on in-room television sets.

Los Angeles and Southern California Time and Area Codes

California is on Pacific Time, or three hours behind Eastern Time. For example, when it is 3:00 P.M. in New York City or Toronto, it is noon in Los Angeles.

The area code for Los Angeles, Hollywood, Beverly Hills, Santa Monica, and Long Beach is 213; for Anaheim, Costa Mesa, and Garden Grove, 714; for Santa Barbara, 805; and for Palm Springs and San Diego, 619.

Important Telephone Numbers

Police, Fire, Medical, Dial 911
Doctor Referral Service, Monday through Friday from 9:00 A.M. to 4:45 P.M., (213) 483–6122
Regional Poison Information Center, operates twenty-four hours a day, (213) 484–5151
Time, (213) 853–1212
Weather, (213) 554–1212
Community Services Information, operates twenty-four hours a day, (800) 242–4612
Traveler's Aid Twenty-four-hour "Infoline," (213) 686–0950
Beach Conditions, (213) 378–8471
Highway Conditions, (213) 626–7231

Law and Order in Los Angeles

No doubt you have seen enough movies and television shows portraying the violent, seamy side of Los Angeles and have read stories about the gangs and the wide assortment of dangerous persons inhabiting the metropolitan area. There is a great deal of violence in Los Angeles. It is seamy in certain parts. There are people, both unfortunate poor and just plain whacko ones, who live on the streets. The mean gangs exist, and so do the dangerous persons.

Now, the truth of the matter having been stated, there is this to think about: Considering its size, Greater Los Angeles is no more violent or unsavory in certain of its sections than any other large metropolitan area in the United States. It is unlikely you will experience trouble, unless you are in the wrong place at the wrong time, such as walking in an unfamiliar area or neighborhood at night or in certain other areas during daylight. If you are looking for drugs and impromptu sex, you will find them without great inconvenience, but beware of the consequences, such as AIDS.

The city of Los Angeles, the other communities of Los Angeles County, and the cities of Orange County have some of the finest and most professional law enforcement agencies in the country. They do an excellent job in protecting the citizens of and visitors to this metropolitan area. If you have any concern about your well-being in Greater Los Angeles, call the police for assistance (Dial 911) or seek advice from your hotel concierge or guest relations person before you tour or visit unfamiliar areas.

You must be at least twenty-one years of age to purchase alcoholic beverages in California. Do not drink and then drive; for your safety on the road and that of others, bring along a nondrinking designated driver. It is against the law to buy and be served liquor between 2:00 and 6:00 A.M. Packaged alcoholic beverages can be purchased in liquor stores, markets, department stores, and large drugstores. If you drive and drink, expect to be dealt with harshly by the law.

Southern California Weather

The weather in Greater Los Angeles and the rest of Southern California is usually perfect—sunny, mild, dry, pleasant, around 80 degrees F.

Rain falls between November and March, and fierce Santa Ana winds occasionally blow from east to northeast during this period.

Winter temperatures can dip below 50 degrees F, and snow falls at higher levels and in the mountains. During the summer, temperatures can go well above 100 degrees F. But the air is dry, lacking stifling humidity. The beaches of Southern California and cool Pacific waters are nearby to cool you off. The air in Los Angeles is clear on many days, but there are occasional atmospheric inversions wherein smog-saturated air (mostly pollutants emitted by countless vehicles on the roads) is trapped in the topographical bowl that the mountains form around the flatlands of Greater Los Angeles. The infamous Los Angeles smog usually occurs on hot, windless days but dissipates when the winds again blow.

Although Greater Los Angeles and the rest of Southern California do have a few days of lousy weather, they also have more perfect ones throughout the year than most other regions of the United States and Canada do.

What to Wear

Both the pleasant, sunny climate and the laid-back life-style of Greater Los Angeles and Southern California are nonautocratic when it comes to clothing. Wear whatever is comfortable and appropriate for the season, be it Rodeo Drive expensive or bargain-store chic. Casual, colorful, exotic, and creative are the only guidelines. Southern California's fashion attitudes often create popular trends for the rest of the country.

Men are required to wear jackets and ties only at certain well-bred restaurants. Women should bring a gorgeous cocktail dress or a sexy floor-length version for special occasions. Do not leave home without your bathing suit; if you do, though, just about every clothing store sells them and in current styles perhaps not available back home. Also bring a sweater and a light jacket for cool nights, as well as a raincoat. Sunglasses are not just fashion statements in Southern California; they are essential to protect your vision, particularly while driving or out on the beach. Also bring or purchase sunscreen lotion for your loafing time on the beach.

Religious Services

Churches, synagogues, mosques, and temples are located in just about every neighborhood in Greater Los Angeles. Each has its mix of places of worship, reflecting the religious preferences of its citizens. Hotels and resorts offer a list of local places of worship for the convenience of their guests. Several special places of worship, such as the Crystal Cathedral, Wayfarers Chapel, and the Spanish Colonial Missions, are described in this guide.

Banking and Credit Cards

Normal banking hours in Greater Los Angeles and for the rest of California are from 9:00 A.M. to 3:00 P.M. Pacific Time. Many banks have extended hours on certain weekdays and special hours on Saturday. Automatic Teller Machines (ATMs) are located just about everywhere. You are advised not to use outdoor ATMs at night in isolated or unfamiliar areas; ask your hotel concierge or guest relations person for safe, convenient locations. Foreign currencies can be exchanged for U.S. dollars at the Bank of America at 525 South Flower Street in downtown Los Angeles or at Los Angeles Currency Exchange at Tom Bradley Terminal at LAX. Many major hotels will also exchange currencies.

Major credit cards (Visa, MasterCard, and their international equivalents; American Express; Discover; etc.) and major traveler's checks are widely accepted by businesses and services in Greater Los Angeles and Southern California.

Free TV Show Tickets

One of the most popular attractions of Los Angeles is the opportunity to be part of the audience at the taping or live broadcast of a television show. Do not purchase tickets to television shows. Television-show tickets are free and readily available from many different sources.

Following are the major sources of free tickets to TV shows:

NBC Shows, 3000 West Alameda Avenue, Burbank 91523; (818) 840–3537. The ticket office is open Monday through Friday from 8:30 A.M. to 5:00 P.M. and Saturday and Sunday from 9:30 A.M. to 4:00 P.M. Tickets to popular shows are available on a first come, first served basis and do not guarantee admission. Tickets for Johnny Carson's *The Tonight Show* must be obtained through the mail several weeks in advance. For more information on attending *The Tonight Show,* call the above number.

ABC Shows, 4151 Prospect Avenue, Hollywood 90027; (213) 557–4396. Ticket window is open Monday through Friday, 9:00 A.M. to 5:00 P.M.

CBS Shows, 7800 Beverly Boulevard, Los Angeles 90036; (213) 852–4002. Ticket window open Monday through Friday, 9:00 A.M. to 5:00 P.M.; Saturday and Sunday, 10:00 A.M. to 5:00 P.M.; closed holidays.

Audiences Unlimited, ticket office located at Fox TV Center, 5764 Sunset Boulevard, Los Angeles 90028; (818) 506–0043. Open Monday through Friday, 8:00 A.M. to 4:00 P.M. This agency provides free tickets to top TV shows produced by the networks and others.

Paramount TV Audience Shows, 860 North Gower Street, Hollywood 90038; (213) 468–5575. Tickets are available at Paramount Visitor Center, Monday through Friday, 10:00 A.M. to 4:00 P.M.

You can also pick up free television show tickets at Universal Studios Tour, outside Mann's Chinese Theatre, and at the Greater Los

Angeles Visitor and Convention Bureau information centers downtown and in Hollywood.

Special Events

For more information on these annual events and other special
events, contact the Greater Los Angeles Visitor and Convention
Bureau, 695 South Figueroa Street, Los Angeles 90071; (213) 689–
8822.

JANUARY
Tournament of Roses Parade, Pasadena, January 1 (January 2 if
New Year's Day falls on a Sunday). The year 1989 was the
hundredth anniversary of an American classic celebration, the
annual Tournament of Roses Parade. This nationally televised
parade—seen by at least three-hundred million people in
more than sixty countries—features creative floats and sym-
phonic marching bands. If you wish to see the parade in person
and are coming from a distance, be sure to book your accommodations in the Los Angeles area well in advance. For
information, call (213) 681–3724 or (818) 449–ROSE, a twenty-
four-hour, year-round hot line of pre-recorded messages.
Rose Bowl Game, Pasadena, January 2. Tickets for this premier
collegiate football bowl game are just about impossible to get
unless you have some good connections or are willing to pay
blood money to scalpers
International Folk Dance Festival, Los Angeles, early January
Oshogatsu—Japanese New Year celebration—Los Angeles, early
January
Three Kings Celebration, traditional Mexican Christmas celebration,
Universal City, early January
Bonsai Show, Arcadia, late January

FEBRUARY
Chinese New Year Celebration, Los Angeles, early February
Black History Month, Los Angeles, through February
Miss Chinatown Beauty Pageant, Los Angeles, early February
Southern California Boat Show, Los Angeles, early February
Los Angeles Children's Mini-Marathon, Los Angeles, mid-February

TRAVEL INFORMATION

MARCH
Annual City of Los Angeles Marathon, Los Angeles, early March
Annual Kite Festival, Redondo Beach, mid-March
Annual Saint Patrick's Day Parade, Los Angeles, mid-March
Swallows Day Parade, Mission of San Juan Capistrano, mid-March
Blessing of the Animals, El Pueblo de Los Angeles Historic Park in Los Angeles, late March
Annual Academy Awards (Motion Picture Arts and Sciences), Los Angeles, late March

APRIL
Toyota Pro-Celebrity Race, Long Beach, early April
Hanamatsuri—Buddha's birthday celebration, Little Tokyo in Los Angeles, early April
Cherry Blossom Festival, Los Angeles, late April
Annual Renaissance Pleasure Faire, Los Angeles, late April

MAY
Cinco de Mayo, Mexican festival, Los Angeles, early May
California Tour, bicycle time trials, downtown Los Angeles and Hollywood, early May
Queen Mary Jazz Festival, Long Beach, mid-May
Highland Gathering and Scottish Games, Costa Mesa, late May

JUNE
Feria de Los Ninos—Festival of the Children—Los Angeles, early June
Los Angeles Jewish Festival, Los Angeles, early June
Annual Grand Irish Faire and Music Festival, Burbank, mid-June
Gay Pride Festival, Los Angeles, late June
Santa Monica Pier Kite Festival, Santa Monica, late June

JULY
Summer Concert Season at the Hollywood Bowl, Hollywood, July to September
Orange County Fair, Costa Mesa, mid-July
Garlic Festival, West Hollywood, mid-July
American Boating Jubilee, Long Beach, late July
International Surf Festival, Hermosa Beach, Manhattan Beach, Redondo Beach, and Torrance, late July

TRAVEL INFORMATION

AUGUST
Annual Nisei Week—Japanese festival—Los Angeles, early to mid-August

Seaside Lagoon Sand Castle Design Competition, Redondo Beach, mid-August

Annual Taste of Los Angeles—cuisine and entertainment festival—Santa Monica, mid-August to mid-September

Shakespeare Festival, Los Angeles, late August

SEPTEMBER
Los Angeles Birthday Celebration, Los Angeles, early September

Beverly Hills Fashion Summit, Beverly Hills, early September

Annual Oktoberfest, Torrance, early September to late October

Los Angeles Country Fair—reputed to be the world's largest—Pomona, mid-September to early October

Mexican Independence Day Celebration, Los Angeles, mid-September

OCTOBER
Day of the Drum Festival, Watts section of Los Angeles, early October

Los Angeles Garden Show, Arcadia, late October

Southern California Sail and Power Boat Show, Long Beach, late October

NOVEMBER
Dia de Las Muertos—Day of the Ancestors celebration—Los Angeles, early November

Annual Beverly Hills Pageant, Beverly Hills, late November

Old Pasadena Celebration, Pasadena, late November

Hollywood Christmas Parade, Hollywood, late November

DECEMBER
Camellia Show, Arcadia, early December

Annual Beverly Hills 10K Race and 5K Waiter and Waitress Race, Beverly Hills, early December

International Contemporary Art Fair, Los Angeles, early to mid-December

Los Angeles Harbor Christmas Afloat, Los Angeles Harbor, early December

Christmas Boat Parade, Marina del Rey, early December

3

Hollywood:
The Entertainment Capital
of the World

Here are a few of the thousands of words that best describe Hollywood: Lights! Camera! Action! Imagination. Fantasy. Creative excellence. Suspense. Adventure. Romance. Comedy. Cartoons. Thrillers. Cowboys and Indians. Crime and justice. Socko! Boffo! The Academy Awards. Black and white. Color. Silent screen. Talkies. Star quality. Mega-stars and blooming starlets. Universal. MGM. Columbia. Walt Disney. United Artists. Paramount. Warner Brothers. NBC. CBS. ABC.

Also: Barbra Streisand, Michael Jackson, Bob Hope, Johnny Carson, Katharine Hepburn, Carol Burnett, Cary Grant, Clark Gable, Vivien Leigh, Grace Kelly, John Wayne, Frank Sinatra, Gary Cooper, George Burns, Humphrey Bogart, Judy Garland, Errol Flynn, Clint Eastwood, Henry Fonda, Fred Astaire, Bette Midler, James Stewart, Marilyn Monroe, Spencer Tracy, Ronald Reagan, Paul Newman, Jack Nicholson, Zasu Pitts, Robert DeNiro, Elizabeth Taylor, Meryl Streep, Eddie Murphy, Tom Cruise, Robert Redford, Dennis Quaid, Shirley MacLaine, William Hurt, Gregory Peck.

And: bit players and walk-ons, character actors, special-effects wizards, composers, writers, producers, directors, camera-persons, sound technicians, stuntmen and women, film editors, costume designers, makeup artists, hair designers, exhibitors, public relations flacks, gossip columnists. Hollywood is all this individually and in the aggregate but also so much more.

There is not one Hollywood but three of them.

The first Hollywood is an actual geographic entity located to the west of downtown Los Angeles, bordered by Wilshire Boulevard to the south and the Ventura Freeway on the north. The Hollywood Freeway slices a diagonal through its heart, and Hollywood Boulevard and Sunset Boulevard are two famous streets, as are Vine and Vermont. Paramount and Warner are the only major studios left in Hollywood, although all the others are located close by, on its fringes, in Burbank, Universal City, and Culver City.

This real place called Hollywood has Mann's Chinese Theatre with its foot and handprints of the past and current stars cast in cement, the Hollywood Walk of Fame with the names of stars set into the sidewalks of Hollywood Boulevard and Vine Street, the famous Hollywood Sign that originally hawked a real estate development, a movie star wax museum, recording studios, and laboratories and workshops that provide technical services to the movie, record, and television industries.

Hollywood and Sunset boulevards are, on any given day, packed tooth and jowl with tourist stargazers furtively searching for famous faces riding in Rolls-Royces or stretch limos, wearing furs and gems equal in worth to the gross national product of many nations. This Hollywood no longer exists, except during premieres of new movies at Mann's Chinese Theatre or at other Los Angeles venues for Academy Award ceremonies when the glitter and magic returns and dazzles, if only briefly. The streets of Hollywood are also populated by unknowns from every corner of North America, all hoping that they too will suddenly be discovered and become rich and famous. This being plucked out of obscurity almost never happens, but it occasionally does, and so the hope and the possibility of outrageous success are perpetuated into new generations.

There are also strange and pathetic street people here during daylight, and the even more unsavory types come out of their dismal dens when darkness commands the streets. You see the disillusioned, the despairing, the exploited, and the exploiters. And then there are the anonymous saints, regular persons with extraordinary virtues who try to comfort and, if possible, salvage some of this rejected humanity.

Hollywood and Sunset boulevards are streets of reputable shops selling souvenirs, books, and the latest fashions for the young. Here are Frederick's of Hollywood, with its Babylonian inventory of erotic lingerie, and pawnbrokers for those with cash-empty pockets. Here also are the dangerous persons, sellers of mind-, body-, and soul-destroying crack, angel dust, cocaine, and pot, and the peddlers—slave masters—of young female and male flesh to satisfy the perversions of the soulless.

Hollywood the real place is both wonderful and evil, both ordinary and bizarre, just like your own hometown. But when it comes to Hollywood, these aspects are perceived by outsiders as magnified far beyond their true proportions. This unique enclave within America is always seen as King Kong, larger than life, when it is in fact a relatively small place, and as a powerful, magnetic mecca, far more important than it actually is. You will find Hollywood fascinating, enjoyable, and safe during the day, but be streetwise when touring on foot at night, just as you would back home.

The second Hollywood consists of the movie, recording, and television industries that employ more than two hundred thousand persons in Greater Los Angeles, from the actors you see on screen to the workers cleaning up messes after the cameras have stopped shooting. This Hollywood is based in the nearby Burbank area, and in Universal City, as well as in on-location shooting throughout Los Angeles County. The Los Angeles telephone Yellow Pages are filled with the names of production companies and the thousands of services that support this multibillion-dollar industry. The Hollywood of the studios, workshops, offices, and laboratories is indeed a factory town where the product produced is entertainment, often extraordinary entertainment.

The people who make the movies are among our nation's brightest and talented. Some critics say it is a shame that so much brains and talent is devoted to such a mindless, unpredictable business, yet life would indeed be drab without the more memorable movies and television shows that entertain, inspire, and inform us. In my opinion, the intelligent, able individuals who have pursued these positive goals have contributed as much value to our society as people in any other honorable profession have.

The third reality of Hollywood is not as a place but as a state of mind. It is a truism that motion picture and television show production is synonymous with Hollywood, regardless of whether it takes place in Canada, Britain, France, or another country. When a movie is shot in Peoria or Toronto, people in those places think "Hollywood": wherever a movie is shot, people think "Hollywood." When people in distant lands learn about America, they discover it through Hollywood-produced movies and television more so than from the printed media or classroom teachings. The image of America as a place where the streets are paved with gold . . . or as a drug-ridden, violent society . . . or as somewhere an individual can be free and succeed—all these facets, the accurate and the distorted, have been projected to the world by Hollywood.

The American motion picture industry began not in frenetic, zany Hollywood, California, but in the West Orange, New Jersey, laboratory of Thomas A. Edison, the famed inventor. In 1888 Edison said, "I am working on an invention that does for the eye what the phonograph [which he also invented] does for the ear." In 1891 Edison developed his first kinetograph, an early motion picture viewing device, and in 1893 he filed a patent for the motion picture camera. At his New Jersey laboratory he also built the world's first motion picture studio, known as the Black Maria, a "revolving photograph building" named for the police paddy wagons of his time. From the mind of this genius a fabulous entertainment and educational medium was born that, for better or worse, affects our lives to this day and beyond.

In its early days the American motion picture industry was almost exclusively centered in New Jersey and New York State. The financing of movies continues to be done on Wall Street and in other money markets. Some silent pictures, such as the still exciting-to-watch *Perils of Pauline,* were shot in upstate New York, in Ithaca, near Cornell University. In nearby Rochester the Eastman Kodak Company was the pioneer in inventing and producing the special film required and consumed in vast quantities by this new industry. Kodak is still the leader in creating and making stock films for motion pictures.

Motion picture production moved from the East Coast to the Los Angeles area in the early 1900s because shooting pictures in Southern California cost less: There was almost continuous sunshine throughout the year for photography; taxes were low or yet nonexistent; the area was a refuge for moviemakers escaping creditors; and it was an immensely pleasant part of the country in which to live and work.

Hollywood itself came into existence in 1887 as a temperance community, one dedicated to prohibiting the evils of booze, an attempt at virtue that did not last long. Before the movie people took over, the hills and flats of Hollywood were largely a real estate development. The famous Hollywood Sign advertised housing lots, not a show-biz mecca. The first Hollywood motion picture was made

HOLLYWOOD

in a barn near Sunset Boulevard and Vine Street in 1910. From these beginnings "Tinsel Town" was born.

The famous Hollywood Sign, 50-foot-high letters located on the slope of Mount Lee, originally advertised a housing development. For many years, however, it has meant to people around the world that Hollywood is the movie and television capital of the world. When you are touring Hollywood you won't fail to see the sign, which originally cost $21,000 but is now a priceless landmark.

Not long after the early moviemakers rooted themselves in Los Angeles, the big studios came into being, and they controlled everything, from making pictures to the hometown theaters that showed them. The actors—such as Clark Gable and Vivian Leigh, the leads in *Gone with the Wind*—were contract players, each viewed as studio property, no different from any tangible asset but, of course, considerably more valuable. The studios had powerful control over their stars lives, even changing their names to make them more memorable in the minds of movie ticket buyers, like you and me. Here are a few famous name changers: George M. Letz became George Montgomery, Eddie Albert was born Edward Heimberger, Nick Perido became Perry Como, Julie Andrews was Julia Wells, Danny Kaye was David D. Kaminski, Jennifer Jones was Phyllis Isley, Judy Garland was Frances Gumm, and Joan Crawford was Billie Cassin.

Motion pictures were created around the stars, and public relations made the stars more famous around the world than actual saints and real heroes. Each studio was a family. When a family member, such as a top box-office star, got himself or herself into a mess that could blow up into a national scandal, the studio provided a cover-up. It had a valuable investment to protect, one worth millions of dollars in profits. Hollywood has plenty of stories of unsolved murders and unspeakable acts hinting at big names but lacking hard evidence to finger the guilty.

When courts forced the breakup of the studios—that is, their total control of the business—in the 1960s—these tight, autocrat-dominated moviemaking families were dissolved. A new era in the economics of the business had arrived; so had competition from television. The contract players, writers, and other talents became free-lancers. Although they now had more control over their personal and professional lives, they lost studio protection and promotion, as well as predictability of work.

Into this void came the talent agent. Some call this occupation pimping. Others, the majority in the business, say it is honest brokering between available talent and producers who need a certain mix of talent for their pictures. Talent agents have been part of the entertainment industry for almost as long as there have been persons wanting to perform before audiences for money. Today the talent agent, usually a member of a large organization like William Morris or else running a small shop in Malibu, has become a vital, powerful mover and shaker in the industry.

If you have acting or writing talent and want to get into the business, it is difficult to do so without an agent. Agents have contradictory dispositions: They want you, but they have protected themselves against you because they do not know you. At any rate, Hollywood is well populated with agents whose business can only prosper with the constant infusion of new talent. Both the Screen Actors Guild (213–465–4600) and the Writers Guild of America (213–550–1000) will provide you with lists of agents, many of whom are receptive to new people with potential star quality. If you want to be in the movies, television shows, or advertising commercials, casting agents need people as walk-ons (for bit parts). Call the Screen Actors Guild for more information, or read *Daily Variety*, *Hollywood Reporter*, and *Billboard Magazine*, the trade journals of the entertainment business.

The best way for you to "go Hollywood" is just for the fun of it. Enjoy everything during your visit. Imagine yourself bigger than life—a movie star—but leave the star business part of it to that one in a million who might get a lucky break and make it to a mansion in Bel Air. Return home safe, and enjoy the memories of your trip. Still, maybe you or possibly even I are that one in a million.

"Writers Guild!"

"Screen Actors Guild!"

"May we help you?"

"Could you please send me a list of agents. I have this great idea for a movie, a terrific blockbuster. . . . I can act like Lawrence Olivier and I look like Gary Cooper . . . and my sister, Zasu, is another Meryl Streep. . . "

Both the magical and the real worlds of Hollywood can be experienced with delight at the following attractions.

This famous Hollywood intersection is a focal point of the Entertainment Capital. The Capitol Record Company offers tours showing how records are made.

Universal Studios Hollywood

Location: 100 Universal City Plaza, Universal City; via the Hollywood Freeway from downtown Los Angeles, at Lankershim or Cahuenga exit.
Telephone Information: Guest information, (818) 508–9600.
Mailing Address: 100 Universal City Plaza, Universal City 91608.
Cost: Admission price includes Tram Tour, all shows and attractions. Special prices for children and seniors. Universal's Celebrity Pass gives you unlimited visits for one full year, as well as access to special events; discounts at hotels, restaurants, car-rental companies, and other attractions; and many other benefits.
Hours of Operation: Summer and holidays, 8:30 A.M. to 5:00 P.M.; rest of the year, Monday through Friday from 9:30 A.M. to 3:30 P.M. and Saturday and Sunday from 9:30 A.M. to 3:30 P.M.
Peak Visiting Periods: Summer months, school vacations, weekends, and holidays.
Time to See Everything: One full day.
Guest Amenities: There are restaurants, snack shops, and stores here. Nearby are hotels, more restaurants, shops, and other attractions. An eighteen-theater complex showing the latest films is also part of the Universal Studios Hollywood grounds.

WHAT TO SEE AND DO

Until the Universal Studios Tour opened to delight the public, you had to have real pull with a big shot in the movie biz to get to see how pictures are made; studio production lots in Hollywood were strictly off limits to the public. Today, however, Universal Studios Hollywood not only shows you how it is done but also lets you share in the excitement of making movies.

This tour takes you through the world's largest motion picture and television studio. Universal Studios Hollywood is a fascinating, thrilling, behind-the-scenes journey through the magic world of movie and television production. As you travel on a special tram, you come face to face with giant King Kong and tooth to tooth with the fearsome shark from the movie *Jaws.*

On this fabulous tour and at the shows you experience the Collapsing Bridge, the Parting of the Red Sea, the Flash Flood, the Battle of Galactica fought with lasers, the Burning House, the Doomed Glacier Expedition, the Adventures of Conan, and the *Miami Vice* Action Spectacular. One of the tour's newest attractions is Earthquake: The Big One, where visitors feel, hear, and see a terrifying, 8.3-magnitude California earthquake as predicted by Universal's own Nostradamus.

You become a space age actor in the *Star Trek* Adventure. You also see sets from many classic movie and television shows, such as *All Quiet on the Western Front, The Sting, Back to the Future, Simon and Simon,* and *Murder, She Wrote.*

The tour also includes the Sword and Action Spectacular, the Western Stunt Show, and the Special Effects Stage. At the Entertainment Center you see stuntmen and women do their tricks and learn about remarkable special effects created by technology and imagination. The Animal Actors Stage has Sunshine the chimp and other animal stars that show you their exceptional talents.

Actors dressed like Frankenstein and Dracula stroll the lot looking for guests who want to pose with them for pictures. Universal Studios has special entertainment events for the public throughout the year. Call ahead to find out what's happening when you are there.

Disneyland

Location: 1313 Harbor Boulevard, Anaheim; off the Santa Ana Freeway at the Harbor Boulevard exit; about forty-five minutes from downtown Los Angeles.

Telephone Information: Guest Relations, (714) 999–4565. Walt Disney Travel Company, (800) 854–3104 in the United States and Canada; information on vacation packages and reservations for Disneyland and other California destinations.

Mailing Address: Walt Disney Travel Company, P.O. Box 3232, Anaheim 92803.

Cost: One-, two-, and three-day Passports allow admission to the park and its attractions. Passports for children ages three through twelve are priced lower.

Hours of Operation: Open every day of the year. Park opens at 9:00 A.M. during weekends and other peak periods and closes in the late evening. Normal hours during off-peak periods are from 10:00 A.M. to 6:00 P.M. For exact hours for your visit, call (714) 999–4565 or (213) 626–8605.

Peak Visiting Periods: School vacations, summer months, weekends, holiday periods. During peak times, be prepared to wait in long lines at popular attractions.

HOLLYWOOD

Time to See Everything: About two days during peak periods. One full day during off peak.

Guest Amenities: Disneyland offers a number of guest services—restaurants, snack places, first aid, lost and found, kennels, auto and RV parking, strollers, lockers, shops, and souvenir stands. Clustered around or near Disneyland are many Anaheim area hotels, motels, restaurants, shops, and attractions.

WHAT TO SEE AND DO

In the 1950s Walt Disney, the moviemaking genius who created Mickey Mouse and other favorite cartoon characters, opened Disneyland, his first family entertainment park. From the beginning Disneyland was an astounding success. It allowed children and adults to enter the fabulous Magic Kingdom, with its Sleeping Beauty Castle centerpiece, and experience the joy of an enchanted world of fun and imagination. Once inside this special world, you do forget, for the time being, your daily cares and enjoy everything. Today the Disney entertainment park success story continues, with Disneyland here in Southern California; Walt Disney World Resort in Orlando, Florida; Walt Disney World in Japan; and a new entertainment park being built in France.

This, the original Disney entertainment park, provides a wholesome and diverting environment for all ages, from tots to older folks. In contrast to the sprawling Orlando resort, Disneyland is within a large but compact area and divided into seven theme districts, such as Fantasyland, Tomorrowland, Adventureland, Frontierland, New Orleans Square, Main Street, and Bear Country. Many of the attractions in these theme areas are based on Walt Disney movies or television shows, such as *Swiss Family Robinson* and *Davy Crockett.* Transportation in the park is provided by the monorail system, the Disneyland Railroad, old-time autos, and horse-drawn vehicles. Wear comfortable shoes and clothing for touring Disneyland on foot.

Following is a sampling of the major attractions at Disneyland.

Main Street, at the entrance, is a re-creation of a turn-of-the-century American small town, exuding the nostalgia of that somewhat-more-innocent period. There are all sorts of interesting shops here, as well as the Abraham Lincoln audio-animatronics show at the Opera House. A robotic Lincoln comes alive and inspires us with his ideals.

Frontierland is where you will find the Golden Horseshoe Jamboree show, the Big Thunder Mountain Railroad thrill ride, and the *Mark Twain* Mississippi River sternwheeler.

Adventureland offers the exciting Jungle Cruise, the Swiss Family Robinson tree house, and the Enchanted Tiki Room show.

Bear Country features Disney cartoon bear characters in their rollicking show and Davy Crockett's Explorer Canoes, which take you on the Rivers of America.

New Orleans Square has the popular Pirates of the Caribbean ride and the spooky Haunted Mansion.

Fantasyland is the site of the lovely Sleeping Beauty Castle, the exciting Matterhorn thrill ride, the heartwarming It's a Small World ride, movie cartoon character rides such as Mr. Toad's Wild Ride, and Videopolis, a nighttime dancing place.

Tomorrowland offers Mission to Mars, Submarine Voyage, the *Captain EO* 3-D movie starring Michael Jackson, and Space Mountain, an exciting thrill ride.

New Disneyland attractions include Star Tours at Tomorrowland, based on the *Star Wars* movie, and Splash Mountain in Bear Country, the largest flume ride in the world.

At various Disneyland locations you will find street entertainers, musicians, singers, shows, and concerts. For example, Dixieland jazz is played in New Orleans Square and rock concerts are held at Tomorrowland Terrace. At 8:50 and 11:00 P.M. every evening during the summer Disneyland stages its glittering Electric Light Parade of floats and Disney cartoon characters marching down Main Street. The 8:50 P.M. parade is topped off at 9:30 P.M. with an awesome fireworks display. Special events and live entertainments occur throughout the year at Disneyland.

Other Tours and Attractions

BURBANK STUDIOS VIP TOUR

4000 Warner Boulevard, Burbank; (818) 954–1744. Admission charge includes escorted tour. Open Monday through Friday, 10:00 A.M. to 2:00 P.M.; extended hours during the summer; closed holidays.

Burbank Studios is home to Warner Brothers and Columbia Pictures. The escorted tour shows you the many fascinating aspects of movie and television production, including, when possible, actual films in the making.

HOLLYWOOD

HOLLYWOOD ON LOCATION
8644 Wilshire Boulevard, Beverly Hills; (213) 659–9165. Fee covers list of film-shooting locations and map. "Location List" is published daily at 9:30 A.M.

    The daily Location List tells you where in the metro area and at what time movie and television shows are being filmed. Filming usually starts early in the morning and can continue until late in the evening, and so you have plenty of time to see the action and the star players. This is a self-guided driving tour, assisted by the Location List and map. Be sure to get the current list, since locations and filming times change daily.

NBC STUDIO TOUR
3000 West Alameda Avenue, Burbank; (818) 840–3537. Admission charge for studio tour; free tickets for television shows. Continuous tours operate daily from 9:00 A.M. to 4:00 P.M. on weekdays, from 10:00 A.M. to 4:00 P.M. on Saturday, and from 10:00 A.M. to 2:00 P.M. on Sunday. Call ahead for television show schedule.

    The NBC Studio Tour is the best attraction for seeing how television shows are produced. You get the complete behind-the-scenes look, including special effects. You also get to go on camera and, through special effects, appear on a television monitor soaring as Superman toward the famous Hollywood Sign.

CBS TELEVISION CITY
7800 Beverly Road, Los Angeles; (213) 852–4002 for tickets to CBS television shows. Free. Call ahead for show schedule.

    At Television City you can be part of the audience at popular CBS shows while they are in production.

ABC ENTERTAINMENT CENTER
2020–2040 Avenue of the Stars, Century City; (213) 556–3096; for tickets to ABC television shows call (213) 557–4396 or (213) 557–7777. Free. Call ahead for television show schedule and locations.

    ABC Entertainment Center has the Shubert and Cineplex Odeon theaters, plus many excellent restaurants, nightclubs, and shops.

PARAMOUNT TELEVISION AUDIENCE SHOWS
780 North Gower Street, Hollywood; (213) 468–5575. Free. Call ahead for television show schedule.

HOLLYWOOD

Paramount operates a major movie and television show production facility. You can be in the audience of new television shows in development and those currently being seen on home sets.

ACADEMY OF MOTION PICTURE ARTS AND SCIENCES

8949 Wilshire Boulevard, Beverly Hills; (213) 278–8990; library (213) 278–4313. Free. Open Monday, Tuesday, Thursday, and Friday from 9:00 A.M. to 5:00 P.M.; closed Wednesday, Saturday, and Sunday.

The eagerly awaited annual Academy Awards for excellence in motion picture achievement are the best-known function of the Academy of Motion Picture Arts and Sciences. Its famous Oscar statuette is the highest honor that can be bestowed on those working in films—actors, directors, writers, composers, makeup and costume designers, and those from the many technical crafts. The public is invited to visit the academy's headquarters and view its exhibits and attend film screenings. Film scholars are welcome to do research in its superb library.

AMERICAN FILM INSTITUTE

2221 North Western Avenue, Hollywood; (213) 856–7600. Free. Call ahead for film-screening times and information for use of the Louis B. Mayer Library.

The Louis B. Mayer Library at the institute has America's premier collection of movie scripts. The Sony Video Center screens classic films for the public and is the site of various movie and television festivals.

MANN'S CHINESE THEATRE COMPLEX

6925 Hollywood Boulevard, Hollywood; (213) 464–8111. Admission charge for seeing latest movies. Open daily from noon to midnight; call for movie schedule.

Previously known as Grauman's Chinese Theatre, Mann's is a world-famous motion picture palace. Here many a new movie premiere has taken place, glittering and star-studded. The premieres still happen here; call the theater for information. On the sidewalk in front of the theater are the foot and handprints of famous motion picture stars and their signatures. No doubt you will find many of your favorites.

GENE AUTRY WESTERN HERITAGE MUSEUM

4700 Zoo Drive, Los Angeles, in Griffith Park, next to the zoo; (213) 667–2000. Admission charge. Open daily, 10:00 A.M. to 5:00 P.M.; closed Monday, Thanksgiving, Christmas, and New Year's Day.

Gene Autry is one of moviedom's great singing/action cowboys, appearing in ninety-five films and selling more than forty million records. The movie industry grew and prospered on cowboy/western films. Audiences could not get enough of them, and Tom Mix, Gene Autry, Roy Rogers, and many others became important stars; even John Wayne played some of his best roles in westerns. These stars' entertaining, moralistic films can still be enjoyed on television.

Gene Autry's intense interest in the American Old West is on display in this excellent and substantial new museum. Its extensive, attractive collection (sixteen thousand artifacts worth more than $20 million) contains historic costumes, firearms, paintings, and documents of cowboys, lawmen, pioneers, and Indians. Here you will see Teddy Roosevelt's Colt revolver, Tom Mix's Stetson, William ("Buffalo Bill") Cody's saddle, and paintings by Frederic Remington and Charles Russell. The exhibits are in seven theme galleries: the Spirit of Discovery portrays the contributions of Spanish, French, and American explorers; The Spirit of Opportunity, the story of the pioneers; and other galleries highlight the Spirit of Conquest, the Spirit of Community, the Spirit of the Cowboy, the Spirit of Romance, and the Spirit of Imagination. A visit here is highly recommended.

THE HOLLYWOOD STUDIO MUSEUM

2100 North Highland Avenue, Hollywood; (213) 874–2276. Admission charge. Open Tuesday through Sunday, 10:00 A.M. to 4:00 P.M; closed holidays.

Housed in the historic deMille barn, where in 1913 the first feature-length film was shot in Hollywood, this museum has exhibits portraying Hollywood's early years in filmmaking.

HOLLYWOOD WAX MUSEUM

6767 Hollywood Boulevard, Hollywood; (213) 462–8860. Admission charge. Open daily from 10:00 A.M. to midnight.

This interesting wax museum contains more than 170 lifelike movie personalities formed out of wax and set against scenes from award-winning films from 1927 to the present.

MOVIELAND WAX MUSEUM

7711 Beach Boulevard, Buena Park, near Disneyland; (714) 552–1154. Admission charge. Open daily; call for exact hours, which vary according to season.

More than two hundred realistic, life-size wax figures of popular movie and television stars are presented in this museum. New figures include Michael Jackson and Sylvester Stallone.

MAX FACTOR MUSEUM

1555 North Highland Avenue, Hollywood; (213) 463–6668. Free. Open Monday through Saturday, 10:00 A.M. to 4:00 P.M.; closed holidays.

Max Factor was the dean of Hollywood makeup artists. His job was to make stars look beautiful or handsome for the uncompromising eye of the camera and thence the big screen viewed by millions around the world. This museum celebrates Max Factor's seventy-five years of achievement in cosmetic makeup for the motion picture industry. Next to the museum is an outlet store where you can buy cosmetics and perfumes for at least 15 percent below retail.

SUNSET STRIP

Not many years ago, this famous section of Sunset Boulevard in West Hollywood had swank nightclubs, such as Ciro's, Trocadero, and Mocambo. Here superstars, starlets, agents, directors, writers, producers, and unknowns, angling for a way to get into the lucrative movie business, came to wine, dine, dance, relax, and show off. The lavish display was for many in the business more important than the wining and dining. Here the gossip columnists reigned and gleefully reported on who was seen with whom. Being seen cozy with the right people could advance a talent's career; being seen with losers could kill it. At the nightclubs scandals were made, but so was true romance. The Strip is still movie-star chic but in different ways. It has become less important in a career promotional sense. Today, many distinctive shops, restaurants, and art galleries line the Strip and cater to the modern tastes of a more diversified clientele.

HOLLYWOOD BOULEVARD

In the past, Hollywood Boulevard was a golden thoroughfare of mansions, expensive stores, and top restaurants. It was also known as the Boulevard of Broken Dreams, because of those who hungered for fame in Hollywood but failed in their try. Today the bou-

HOLLYWOOD

levard has become somewhat tacky but is not without its allures, such as the Walk of Fame, where memorials to close to two thousand stars are set into the sidewalk. Each star honors a person who has achieved distinction in the movies, television, recorded music, radio, or live theater. The Walk of Fame also continues on Vine Street. The corner of Hollywood and Vine was considered special in the glamorous myths and legends of discovering stars from unknowns. The annual Hollywood Christmas Parade, televised throughout North America, takes place on Hollywood Boulevard in late November.

Here also is Mann's Chinese Theatre (6925 Hollywood Boulevard), where glittering movie premieres are held. In front of the theater are the concrete-cast footprints, handprints, and signatures of many stars—Mary Pickford and Douglas Fairbanks were among the first to be so enshrined. Also in this area you will find Frederick's of Hollywood (6608 Hollywood Boulevard), famous purveyor of sexy lingerie; C. C. Brown's Ice Cream (7007 Hollywood Boulevard), which served hot fudge sundaes to the likes of Bob Hope, Judy Garland, and John Wayne; the landmark round tower of Capitol Records (1750 North Vine Street); Hollyhock House (4800 Hollywood Boulevard), designed by Frank Lloyd Wright; and the Egyptian Theatre (6712 Hollywood Boulevard), site of the first Hollywood movie premiere and one of the first of the grand movie palaces. Griffith Observatory in Griffith Park was the location for scenes for the film *Rebel without a Cause* and the site of an extraordinary bust of actor James Dean, who was the lead in that movie. Janes House (6541 Hollywood Boulevard) is the last of the Victorian mansions here. Formerly a private school for the children of Charlie Chaplin, Cecil B. deMille, and other celebrities, Janes House now serves as a visitor information center of the Greater Los Angeles Visitor and Convention Bureau. Stop in here for maps, brochures, and answers to your touring questions.

Here also you will find Larry Edmund's Book Store (6658 Hollywood Boulevard), with the largest collection in Los Angeles of books on the movies and live theater; Hollywood murals (seen as well throughout Los Angeles), giant paintings of people and strange images on the sides of buildings; Musso and Frank's (6667 Hollywood Boulevard), the oldest eatery in Hollywood and the watering hole for writers William Faulkner, Ernest Hemingway, and F. Scott Fitzgerald. The Screen Actors Guild is at 7065 Hollywood Boulevard.

Star Line, located at the Chinese Theatre (6845 Hollywood Boulevard), provides professionally conducted sightseeing tours of

Hollywood attractions and the homes of the stars; call (213) 463–3131 for information. Hollywood on Parade (818–843–3415), a tour service operated by people who work in the movies, will show you locations for films shot in the past and films being shot now. A comprehensive free guide to Hollywood is *Discover the Arts in Hollywood,* available at the Janes House visitor center.

Memorials to Yesterday's Stars

Thanks to movies, our favorite stars always remain as glamorous and fascinating as when we saw them on the silver screen or video. Movie stars in real life are obviously not immortal, but for fans and the curious, their final resting places can be interesting. Many people, for example, come weekly to Westwood Memorial Cemetery to pay homage to Marilyn Monroe. Visits to the cemeteries of the stars need not be maudlin affairs; they can instead present an opportunity to come closer in psychic terms with those who seemed larger than life and who touched us kindly with their talents.

FOREST LAWN MEMORIAL PARK
1712 South Glendale Avenue, Glendale; (213) 254–3131. Free. Open daily, 9:00 A.M. to 5:00 P.M.
    Several decades ago, Forest Lawn was considered an outlandish necropolis. Today, a less puritanical attitude finds Forest Lawn soothing and even joyous. Here the famous deceased reside in lavish tombs as before they resided in grand mansions. Here also their ashes are sequestered in compartments within silent marble palaces whose polished surfaces are dappled with colored light from stained glass. There are statues of saints and of the Lord (the Hall of the Crucifixion and Resurrection) and monuments to our nation's heritage (the Court of Freedom). There are also a museum and a memento shop. Clark Gable and Jean Harlow are among the film greats buried at Forest Lawn.

HOLLYWOOD MEMORIAL CEMETERY
6000 Santa Monica Boulevard, Los Angeles; (213) 469–1181. Free. Open Monday through Friday from 8:00 A.M. to 5:00 P.M. and Saturday and Sunday from 9:00 A.M. to 4:00 P.M.
    Within the peaceful grounds of this cemetery are buried many top film personalities, such as Cecil B. deMille, producer and director of stupendous Hollywood epics; Rudolph Valentino, the hot

lover of the silent screen; Douglas Fairbanks, the swashbuckling hero of romantic adventure films during the silent movie era; Tyrone Power, a popular lead actor of the fifties and sixties; and many other celebrities.

WESTWOOD MEMORIAL CEMETERY
1218 Glendon Avenue, Westwood. Free.

Westwood Memorial Cemetery is best known for having the graves of Marilyn Monroe and Natalie Wood.

4

Greater Los Angeles and Orange County Attractions, Gardens, and Museums of All Kinds

Downtown Los Angeles is a fabulous, not-to-be-missed attraction in itself, offering many interesting and pleasurable experiences. Here, for example, is El Pueblo de Los Angeles National Historic Park, where the city began as a Spanish colonial outpost and mission in the eighteenth century (the settlement was officially founded in 1781). In this area are a number of historic buildings and artifacts, such as Pelanconi House (1855); Sepulveda House (1887); Zanja Madre, a ditch that was the town's first water-carrying system; Avila Adobe, the city's oldest remaining structure; Old Plaza Firehouse (1884); the city's first Masonic temple (1858); Pico House (1870), residence of California's last Mexican governor; and the Church of Our Lady Queen of the Angels, the oldest house of worship in Los Angeles.

The main attraction of El Pueblo de Los Angeles area is Olvera Street, closed to vehicular traffic and running through the center of this unique National Historic Park. Olvera Street is the Los Angeles version of a colorful Mexican *mercado,* or outdoor/indoor market. Along Olvera Street are numerous Mexican gourmet restaurants, shops selling well-made handicrafts from Mexican and California artisans, and Mexican fast-food eateries dispensing tacos by the thousands per hour.

At the center of Olvera Street is Plaza, a broad round open

space where several Mexican festivals take place during the year, such as the Blessing of the Animals (a spring festival before Easter), Cinco de Mayo (the May 5 Mexican holiday), and Los Posadas (a celebration before Christmas). Olvera Street is always busy with people, day or evening. It is especially alive with activity during Friday and Saturday evenings and on Sunday afternoons when the people of Greater Los Angeles (Los Angelenos, as they are sometimes called), as well as visitors from all over the world, enjoy the warmth, color, joy, and music of the city's Mexican heritage.

While in downtown Los Angeles visit Little Tokyo, located between Second and Third streets and off San Pedro Street. The architecture and ambience of Little Tokyo convey the feel of a community in Japan, but it is also a major commercial and cultural area for local Nisei (Japanese Americans). Here you can shop for unique Japanese goods, dine in excellent restaurants, and attend various celebrations held during the year. The deluxe New Otani Hotel is in Little Tokyo, as are the Japanese Village Plaza Mall, the Japanese American Cultural and Community Center, the Japan America Theater, the Nishi Hingwangi Buddhist Temple, the Horikawa Restaurant, and the lovely James Irvine Garden.

The influence of Japan on today's Los Angeles is considerable. Investors in Japan own a large portion of Greater Los Angeles commercial real estate, and Japanese tourists outnumber other groups of visitors to the city.

The Chinese are one of the oldest ethnic communities residing in Los Angeles. They began arriving here in the mid-nineteenth century during California's gold rush period. Chinatown, located just north of El Pueblo de Los Angeles National Historic Park, via North Broadway, bustles with the sights, sounds, and aromas of the exotic Far East, conjuring images of Hong Kong, Taipei, or Shanghai. The best time to visit Chinatown in Los Angeles is during the Chinese New Year celebration, in February, when there are parades, fireworks, and a beauty contest to select Miss Chinatown. Actually, anytime is special in Chinatown, what with all the terrific restaurants plus the infinite number of shops selling curios, handicrafts, herbal medicines, live ducks, and fresh Chinese vegetables.

There is much more to see and do in downtown Los Angeles. Take a tour of the *Los Angeles Times,* one of America's leading newspapers, at 202 West First Street. See Los Angeles from the observation deck high up City Hall, at 200 North Spring Street. Visit the Greater Los Angeles Visitor and Convention Bureau at ARCO Plaza, Sixth and South Flower streets (213–628–3101), for information—offered in several major foreign languages besides English—on attractions, accommodations, dining, and entertainment.

Pershing Square, bordered by Fifth, Sixth, Olive, and Hill streets, is considered the geographical center of downtown Los Angeles. In this vicinity are the Jewelry District, the deluxe Biltmore Hotel on Olive, Los Angeles Theatre Center on Sixth, and Los Angeles Central Library on Fifth. On Second Street is Grand Central Market, an indoor extravaganza of foods for every culture, along with the babble of the world's languages as buyers haggle with sellers.

The impressive Music Center of Los Angeles County, located at First and Hope streets, has three extraordinary theaters—the Dorothy Chandler Pavilion, the Mark Taper Forum, and the Ahmanson Theater. On Figueroa Street, in the Financial District, is the Pacific Stock Exchange, the largest U.S. exchange outside New York City. There is a visitor gallery here so that you can watch the frantic trading action on the floor.

Other downtown attractions include the Garment District, between Los Angeles and San Pedro Street, where you can buy top-label fashions at discount prices; the Wholesale Flower Market, between Seventh and Eighth streets, worth the visit for the colors and fragrances; the Variety Arts Center, on South Figueroa Street, for plays and musicals; the fantastic murals on the sides of buildings throughout downtown; and the surrealistic, futuristic Westin Bonaventure Hotel on South Figueroa Street, used as location in many films and television shows. The Museum of Contemporary Art, on South Grand Avenue, and the Museum of Neon Art, on Traction Street, are major attractions as well.

A short drive to the southwest of downtown Los Angeles, via the Harbor Freeway (Interstate 110), is Exposition Park, bordered by Martin Luther and Exposition boulevards. Within Exposition Park are the Los Angeles Memorial Coliseum, where the 1932 and 1984 Summer Olympic Games took place; the Olympic Arch; the Sports Arena; McDonalds's Olympic Swim Stadium; the New California Museum of Science and Industry; the California Afro-American Museum; and the Los Angeles County Museum of Natural History.

Across Exposition Boulevard is the campus of the University of Southern California (USC), the West Coast's oldest independent, coeducational, nonsectarian institution of higher learning. USC's attractions include Fisher Gallery; the Hancock Memorial Museum; the Arnold Schoenberg Institute; and the Norris Cinema Theater (USC has the best film studies program in the country). On Jefferson

Avenue, across from the USC campus, is the huge, mosquelike Shrine Civic Auditorium, a major venue used for cultural events, Academy Award presentations, and, of course, gatherings of Shriners, glad-handing, philanthropic members of the Masonic fraternity.

Knott's Berry Farm

Location: 8039 Beach Boulevard, Buena Park. Ten minutes from Disneyland; thirty minutes south of downtown Los Angeles via the Santa Ana Freeway.

Telephone Information: Main switchboard, (714) 827–1776. Recorded information, (714) 220–5200.

Mailing Address: 8039 Beach Boulevard, Buena Park 90620.

Cost: Admission provides unlimited use of all rides, shows, and attractions, except the Pan for Gold arcades. Special rates for children ages three through eleven, seniors, expectant mothers, and handicapped guests. No charge for children under three years of age.

Hours of Operation: Open every day. Summer hours: Sunday through Thursday, 10:00 A.M. to 11:00 P.M.; Friday and Saturday, 10:00 A.M. to 1:00 A.M. Winter hours: Monday through Friday, 10:00 A.M. to 6:00 P.M.; Saturday, 10:00 A.M. to 10:00 P.M. ; Sunday, 10:00 A.M. to 7:00 P.M.

Peak Visiting Periods: Summer months, school vacations, long holiday periods, and weekends.

Time to See Everything: One full day.

Guest Amenities: More than sixty dining places, including Mrs. Knott's Chicken Dinner Restaurant, and about sixty shops (Knott's boysenberry jams and jellies are world famous). Parking, foreign-language assistance.

WHAT TO SEE AND DO

Knott's Berry Farm offers hours of great fun for all members of the family—from Old West action in a Ghost Town to entertainment with Snoopy and the Peanuts Gang in Camp Snoopy.

In 1940 Walter Knott began building Ghost Town as a diversion for guests waiting in line at his popular Chicken Dinner Restaurant. He was also an expert botanist, having developed a bigger, better boysenberry for California agriculture. Today Knott's Berry Farm is an American institution offering wholesome family fun.

LOS ANGELES ATTRACTIONS

Knott's offers more than 165 rides, attractions, live shows, restaurants, and shops on 150 acres. Among its thrill rides are Bigfoot Rapids (new), Calico Mine Ride, Corkscrew (having two 360-degree loops), Greased Lightning, Montezuma's Revenge (going from 0 to 55 miles per hour in less than five seconds), Parachute Sky Jump (falling 20 stories), Propeller Spin, Slingshot, and Timberline Twister.

Its major entertainment facilities include Bird Cage Theatre, Cloud 9 Ballroom, Camp Snoopy Theatre, Pacific Pavilion, Toyota Good Time Theatre, Wagon Camp, and Wilderness Dance Hall.

Camp Snoopy is a special children's entertainment area featuring that irrepressible beagle and his *Peanuts* friends. There is a merry-go-round here, as well as a sea lion and dolphin show.

Wild Water Wilderness (new) is a turn-of-the-century river experience featuring the thrilling Bigfoot Rapids ride.

Ghost Town is a re-creation of a nineteenth-century California boomtown, complete with cowboys, rough gunslingers, dance hall girls, and a place for you to pan for gold.

Fiesta Village takes you back to Spanish colonial California in theme and is also packed with thrill rides.

Roaring '20s has the Kingdom of the Dinosaurs ride, putting you near touching distance to the great beasts that once roamed the earth.

During the summer, spectacular fireworks displays take place nightly at 9:45 P.M. at Reflection Lake. Knott's also offers sumptuous musical and ice shows, top-star shows, special 3-D movies, and lots more.

Other Attractions

SIX FLAGS MAGIC MOUNTAIN

26101 Magic Mountain Parkway, Valencia, thirty minutes north of Los Angeles via Interstate 5; (818) 367–2271. Admission price includes all rides, shows, and attractions. During the summer Six Flags Magic Mountain is open daily from 10:00 A.M. to 10:00 P.M. and until midnight on Friday and Saturday; the rest of the year the park is open only on weekends and school holidays.

Six Flags Magic Mountain offers millions of dollars worth of thrill rides and entertainment on 260 acres. Its thrill rides include Colossus, one of the best roller coasters in the country; Revolution, a circular ride at breath-stopping speed; and Roaring Rapids, an exciting white-water river ride. There are shows galore for all ages and, for the little kids, fun rides such as the 6-acre Bugs Bunny World. Among Six Flags Magic Mountain's entertainment offerings is the new Kurt Thomas Gymnastics America show.

LOS ANGELES ZOO
5333 Zoo Drive, Los Angeles, located next to the Gene Autry Museum; (213) 664–1100. Admission charge. Open daily except Christmas.

This world-class zoo contains more than two thousand animals; seventy-eight species are on the endangered list. Exhibits include koalas, a white tiger, gorillas, and orangutans. Also there is a new children's zoo, called Adventure Island, featuring animals from the American Southwest.

RAGING WATERS
111 Via Verde, San Dimas; (714) 592–6453. Admission charge. Open seasonally; call ahead for schedule.

Raging Waters was California's first water amusement park. It features several speed and sled slides, inner-tube rapids, serpentine flumes, and wave and children's pools.

THE QUEEN MARY AND THE SPRUCE GOOSE
Long Beach Harbor at the end of the Long Beach Freeway; (213) 435–3511. An all-day pass allows admission to both the Queen Mary and the Spruce Goose; lower rates for seniors and children; free admission for children under five. Summer season (July 4 through Labor Day), open from 9:00 A.M. to 9:00 P.M., with box office open until 8:00 P.M.; the rest of the year, open from 10:00 A.M. to 6:00 P.M., with box office open until 4:00 P.M.

The famous Cunard ocean liner the *Queen Mary* was purchased by the city of Long Beach in 1967. It is both a tourist attraction and a 390-stateroom hotel (see chapter 6). Special *Queen Mary* exhibitions include ship sound and light shows in the engine room and wheelhouse simulating a collision at sea, a World War II display of the *Queen's* role as a troop ship, and lifeboat demonstrations.

Howard Hughes's famed flying boat, the *Spruce Goose*, is exhibited in a geodesic dome adjacent to the *Queen Mary*. The *Spruce Goose* is an all-wood, 200-ton flying boat that actually flew but did so just one time with enigmatic Howard Hughes, a genuine aviation pioneer, at the controls. The *Goose*, though one of the largest airplanes ever built, was never flown commercially nor rep-

Long Beach Grand Prix
Photo courtesy of Greater Los Angeles
Visitors and Convention Bureau

licated. Visitors get a close look at the cockpit, cargo area, and flight deck. Around the *Goose* are several displays and presentations about the plane and Hughes's extraordinary career in aviation.

CALICO GHOST TOWN

Ghost Town Road at Interstate 15 in Yermo; (619) 254–2122. Admission charge. Open daily, 9:00 A.M. to 5:00 P.M.

If you have a hankering to visit an Old West ghost town, this is the place. Calico Ghost Town was once a bustling silver-mining community. When the ore petered out, the miners, saloon keepers, and dance hall girls moved on to other boomtowns. In its ensuing decrepitude and present restoration, Calico became interesting as a relic from our nation's past. When you come here, use your imagination and see in your mind how it once was. Mine tours are offered. There are campgrounds and eateries here for your convenience.

CABRILLO BEACH MARINE MUSEUM

3720 Stephen White Drive, San Pedro; (213) 548–7562. Admission charge. Open Tuesday through Sunday, 10:00 A.M. to 5:00 P.M. Whale-watching trip information can be obtained by calling (213) 832–4444 (California gray whales migrate from late December through early April).

Many live specimens of marine life are on display, and you can learn how a large aquarium takes care of them. There are also displays of fossils and a large collection of seashells.

MARITIME MUSEUM

Berth 84 in San Pedro; (213) 548–7618. Admission charge. Open Tuesday through Friday, 9:00 A.M. to 5:00 P.M.; Saturday and Sunday, 10:00 A.M. to 5:00 P.M.

This exceptional maritime museum overlooks Los Angeles Harbor and provides a look at the workings of one of the world's major seaports. Its collection includes ship models, such as the ill-fated "Titanic" built from sticks by a young boy; the bridge deck of the cruiser *Los Angeles;* and many other naval artifacts.

CALIFORNIA AFRO-AMERICAN MUSEUM

600 State Street, Los Angeles; (213) 744–7432. Free. Open daily, 10:00 A.M. to 5:00 P.M.

The California Afro-American Museum has exhibits on the culture, history, and experience of blacks in California and throughout the rest of the nation. It also has a research library and museum.

CRAFT AND FOLK MUSEUM

5814 Wilshire Boulevard, Los Angeles; (213) 937–5544. Admission charge. Open Tuesday through Saturday, 11:00 A.M. to 5:00 P.M.

Folk arts and crafts from around the world are exhibited at this museum—textiles, masks, pottery, carvings, paintings, sculpture, art glass, hooked rugs, and toys.

GEORGE C. PAGE MUSEUM OF LA BREA DISCOVERIES

Hancock Park, 5801 Wilshire Boulevard, Los Angeles, next to the Los Angeles County Museum of Art; (213) 936–2230. Admission charge. Open Tuesday through Sunday, 10:00 A.M. to 5:00 P.M.; closed Thanksgiving, Christmas, and New Year's Day.

One hundred tons of fossilized bones representing four hundred species of mammals, birds, reptiles, and fish are on exhibit at this museum—mammoths, mastodons, saber-toothed tigers, and big birds. They were pulled out of sticky tar pools dating from prehistoric times and represent one of the most comprehensive fossil beds ever discovered. The laborious process of finding more fossils continues on at Pit #91.

HOLLYWOOD BOWL MUSEUM

2301 North Highland Avenue, Los Angeles; (213) 850–2059. Free; admission charge for concerts. Open Tuesday through Saturday, 9:30 A.M. to 4:30 P.M.; open daily in summer, until 8:30 P.M. on concert days.

The Hollywood Bowl is the foremost outdoor concert facility in Los Angeles, featuring top performers and orchestras. The museum has interesting exhibits on the performing arts in Los Angeles and at the Hollywood Bowl, as well as a movie on the history of the Hollywood Bowl.

NORTON SIMON MUSEUM

411 West Colorado Boulevard, Pasadena; (818) 449–3730. Admission charge. Open Tuesday through Sunday, noon to 6:00 P.M.

The grandiose Norton Simon Museum displays a broad spectrum of fine art: six centuries of European painting; Indian and Southeast Asian sculpture; and nineteenth- and twentieth-century European sculpture. Among its treasures are works by Degas, Vincent van Gogh, Rembrandt, Matisse, Renoir, Gauguin, and many other masters.

HUNTINGTON LIBRARY, ART GALLERY, AND BOTANICAL GARDENS

1151 Oxford Street, San Marino; (818) 405–2275. Free. Open Tuesday through Sunday, 1:00 to 4:30 P.M; reservations necessary for Sunday visits.

Here you can see Thomas Gainsborough's *Blue Boy.* An extensive, impressive collection of eighteenth- and nineteenth-century British painting and decorative arts is on display in the 1902 mansion of railroad tycoon Henry E. Huntington. The Huntington Library contains more than six hundred thousand books and several million manuscripts. There are 207 acres of grounds here that incorporate several gardens, including a comprehensive cactus garden, and a good restaurant is on the premises.

HOLOGRAPHIC VISIONS

Lower Level, 300 South Grand Avenue, Los Angeles; (213) 687–7171. Admission charge. Closed Monday; open Thursday from 11:00 A.M. to 8:00 P.M. and Saturday, Sunday, Tuesday, Wednesday, and Friday from 11:00 A.M. to 6:00 P.M.

Holography—the use of laser beams to create three-dimensional images, both moving and static—is a fascinating, creative demonstration of advanced science and technology. Exhibitions here underscore the marvels of holography from around the world.

LOS ANGELES CHILDREN'S MUSEUM

310 North Main Street, Los Angeles; (213) 687–8800. Admission charge. Open Wednesday and Thursday from 2:00 to 4:00 P.M. and Saturday and Sunday from 10:00 A.M. to 5:00 P.M.; call for special summer and holiday hours.

This is the place to take kids ages two to twelve for fun with hands-on exhibits—weather reporting in a television studio; a hospital emergency room; a city street with cars, buses, and motorcycles; and lots more.

GRIFFITH OBSERVATORY

2800 East Observatory Road, Griffith Park, Los Angeles; (213) 664–1191. Admission charge for shows. Open Monday through Friday from 1:00 to 10:00 P.M. and Saturday and Sunday from 11:30 A.M. to 10:00 P.M.; during the winter, open Tuesday through Friday from 2:00 to 10:00 P.M., Saturday from 11:30 A.M. to 10:00 P.M., and Sunday from 1:00 to 10:00 P.M.

LOS ANGELES ATTRACTIONS

The observatory offers fascinating shows on the stars, the planets, and the wonders within the infinite cosmos. There is also a dazzling laser light show. Some of the best views of Los Angeles are from here; when the air is smog free, you can see Greater Los Angeles from the mountains to the sea. Although the evening sky and the lights of the city are magical from this vantage point, a visit at night is not recommended (unless you are on a tour or with a group). Scenes from *Rebel without a Cause* and other films were shot at and around the observatory, and a bust of actor and cult hero James Dean is here.

MOUNT WILSON OBSERVATORY
Located in the San Gabriel Mountains, north of Pasadena—take Freeway 210 west to La Canada/Flintridge, exit at Highway 2, and then travel north; (818) 577-1122. Free. Open daily from 10:00 A.M. to 4:00 P.M.
You are welcome to visit the grounds of the observatory and its museum. A free walking tour is given every Sunday at 2:00 P.M. In addition to seeing this famous observatory, the views from the mountain on a clear day are, using Hollywood terminology, "spectacular!"

NATURAL HISTORY MUSEUM OF LOS ANGELES COUNTY
900 Exposition Boulevard, Los Angeles; (213) 744-3414. Admission charge. Open Tuesday through Sunday, 10:00 A.M. to 5:00 P.M.; closed Thanksgiving, Christmas, and New Year's Day.
Here is California's largest single museum. It has the most abundant dinosaur show in the world, as well as a hall of gems and minerals and displays of fossils, plants, and animals.

THE NEW CALIFORNIA MUSEUM OF SCIENCE AND INDUSTRY
Exposition Park at 700 State Drive, Los Angeles; (213) 744-7400. Free. Open daily, 10:00 A.M. to 5:00 P.M.
This museum has undergone a $45 million renovation and expansion. It features exhibits on California industries, a Science Wing, the Mark Taper Hall of Economics and Finance, the Kinsey Hall of Health, and an Aerospace building. The museum also contains a superscreen Mitsubishi IMAX theater (admission charge), a new earthquake exhibit, and various hands-on demonstrations.

SOUTHWEST MUSEUM

234 Museum Drive, Highland Park; (213) 221–2163. Admission charge. Open Tuesday through Saturday, 11:00 A.M. to 5:00 P.M.; Sunday 1:00 to 5:00 P.M.

The oldest museum in Los Angeles. It displays a superb collection of American Indian art and artifacts in four halls: the native people of the Southwest; the Plains; the Northwest Coast; and California. Information is provided on many aspects of early Native American life, from religious rituals to construction of living habitations.

WELLS FARGO HISTORY MUSEUM

333 South Grand Avenue at Wells Fargo Center, Los Angeles; (213) 253–7166. Free. Open every banking day, 9:00 A.M. to 5:00 P.M.

Wells Fargo was one of the major forces in opening and developing the American West by providing postal, transportation, and financial services. Its collection contains more than 130 years of Wells Fargo and western history in five exhibit areas. There are also slide and video presentations.

THE MUSEUM OF NEON ART (MONA)

704 Traction Avenue, Los Angeles; (213) 617–1580. Admission charge. Open Wednesday through Saturday, noon to 5:00 P.M.

MONA is the only museum in the world to focus on all forms of neon, electric, and kinetic art. It also houses a permanent collection of old neon signs.

THE J. PAUL GETTY MUSEUM

17985 Pacific Coast Highway, Malibu; (213) 458–2003. Free. Open Tuesday through Sunday, 10:00 A.M. to 5:00 P.M. Call ahead for parking reservation; no walk-in visitors.

Founded and funded by billionaire J. Paul Getty, this extraordinary museum—its splendid location overlooking the Pacific Ocean—is one of the great art museums of the world. The main gallery is a replica of a first-century Pompeiian villa. The collection includes art from ancient Greece and Italy, French decorative arts, paintings from Western Europe, and more than fifty thousand fine art photographs.

THE MUSEUM OF CONTEMPORARY ART (MOCA)

250 South Grand Plaza at California Plaza, Los Angeles; (213) 621–2766. Admission charge. Open Tuesday, Wednesday, Satur-

day, and Sunday, 11:00 a.m. to 6:00 p.m.; Thursday and Friday, 11:00 a.m. to 8:00 p.m.

MOCA now has a magnificent new gallery building to display its outstanding contemporary art collection. Designed by Arata Izozaki, the facility contains seven levels of galleries, an auditorium, a bookstore, and a sculpture court.

An adjunct gallery, the Temporary (now permanent because of its popularity with the public) Contemporary Museum, is located at 134 and 152 North Central Avenue in Los Angeles (Little Tokyo); call (213) 382–MOCA for information.

LOS ANGELES COUNTY MUSEUM OF ART

5905 Wilshire Boulevard, Los Angeles; (213) 937–2590. Free; admission charge for special exhibitions. Open Tuesday through Friday, 10:00 a.m. to 5:00 p.m.; Saturday and Sunday, 10:00 a.m. to 6:00 p.m.

Within this splendid museum are housed the Ahmanson Gallery of decorative arts, the Armand Hammer Wing for new exhibitions, the Leo S. Bing Center for concerts and film screenings, and the Robert O. Anderson Gallery of contemporary art. The museum also has a remarkable collection of pre-Colombian, Indian, and Southeast Asian art.

WRIGLEY HOUSE AND GARDENS

391 South Orange Grove Boulevard, Pasadena; (818) 449–4100. Free. Open daily, except January 1 and 2.

This was the estate of chewing-gum king William Wrigley. It is also known as the Tournament House, being the headquarters of the Tournament of Roses Association. The impressive mansion is well worth visiting, as are the gardens of roses, camellias, and annuals that grace the grounds.

DESCANSO GARDENS

1418 Descanso Drive, La Canada; (818) 790–5571. Admission charge. Open daily, 9:00 a.m. to 5:00 p.m.; closed Christmas.

Descanso Gardens is a blooming place, located not far from the Rose Bowl. This botanical wonderland consists of 165 acres, 6 miles of walking paths, a Japanese teahouse, more than six hundred varieties of camellia plants, and a four-acre garden of America roses.

LOS ANGELES ATTRACTIONS

LOS ANGELES STATE AND COUNTY ARBORETUM
301 North Baldwin Avenue, Arcadia; (818) 446–8251. Admission charge. Open daily, 9:00 A.M. to 5:00 P.M.; closed Christmas.

The arboretum features 125 acres of botanicals—indigenous plants by geographical region, herbs, orchids, and cycads—and an area displaying historical structures from early California.

SOUTH COAST BOTANIC GARDENS
26300 South Crenshaw Boulevard, Rancho Palos Verdes; (213) 377–0468. Admission charge. Open daily, 9:00 A.M. to 5:00 P.M.

Once an open mine, the refuse-filled pits were planted with botanical species from all the world's continents except Antarctica. South Coast Botanic Gardens, offering horticultural displays, demonstrations, and a gift shop, is an outstanding example of transforming seemingly wasteland into a dazzling flowering oasis.

VIRGINIA ROBINSON GARDENS
1008 Eden Way, Beverly Hills; (213) 276–5367. Admission charge; call for advance visiting reservations. Open Tuesday through Friday, 10:00 A.M. to 3:00 P.M.

This is the oldest home in exclusive Beverly Hills. You are welcome to tour the house and its six acres of gardens and palm groves.

UNIVERSITY OF CALIFORNIA AT LOS ANGELES (UCLA) CAMPUS
308 Westwood Plaza, Westwood; (213) 825–0611. Free access. Open daily. Guided tours offered Monday through Friday, 8:00 A.M. to 5:00 P.M.; call ahead for details.

The lovely campus of UCLA, located in swank Westwood, is a pleasure to visit. Walking tours depart from the Ueboerroth Building. Attractions on campus include the brick Romanesque Powell Library, the Museum of Cultural History, the Dickson Art Center, the Frederick S. Wight Art Gallery, the Franklin Murphy Sculpture Garden, the Pauley Pavilion, Los Angeles Tennis Center, Drake Stadium, the Center for Health Sciences, and the Mathias Botanical Gardens. The main quadrangle, surrounded by brick Romanesque-style buildings, including the Powell Library, has been a location for many movies and television shows.

MISSION SAN FERNANDO REY DE ESPANA
1515 San Fernando Mission Boulevard, Mission Hills; (818) 361–0186. Admission charge. Open daily, 9:00 A.M. to 5:00 P.M.

This Spanish colonial mission, founded in 1791, suffered extensive damage from earthquakes in the nineteenth and twentieth centuries but has been rebuilt to reflect the exquisite architectural and decorative detailing of its original period. Your tour here will show you how the priests and their Indian inhabitants lived, worked, and worshiped.

MISSION SAN GABRIEL ARCHANGEL

537 West Mission Drive, San Gabriel; (818) 282–5191. Admission charge. Open daily, 9:00 A.M. to 4:00 P.M.

Mission San Gabriel was founded in 1771 by Franciscan priests as a kind of self-sustaining utopian Christian environment for themselves and their Indian converts. The concept of a religious-social-economic enclave was a principal impetus for establishing the twenty-one missions along the coast and interior of Alta California. The architectural design of Mission San Gabriel is said to have been influenced by the cathedral of Cordova, Spain. The arches within its bell tower are characteristic of many Spanish colonial mission churches in the American West and Southwest. A museum here has a collection of old vestments, Bibles, and manuscripts.

MISSION SAN JUAN CAPISTRANO

Located south of Costa Mesa via the San Diego Freeway (Interstate 5), between Laguna Beach and Capistrano Beach; (714) 493–1111. Admission charge. Open daily, 7:00 A.M. to 5:00 P.M.

Established in 1776 by Father Junipero Serra, a founder of California and recently elevated by Pope John Paul II toward sainthood, Mission San Juan Capistrano is famous throughout the world for its birds. Each year without fail, the swallows have returned to Capistrano on March 19, the feast of Saint Joseph. Some say it is a miracle; scientists have developed more pragmatic theories. But no one is quite sure why the swallows return precisely on that auspicious day. The mission was destroyed by an earthquake in the early nineteenth century but was rebuilt. A visit here is a reminder of the work of human hands and of faith in a higher intelligence that influences nature beyond our imaginings.

THE CRYSTAL CATHEDRAL

12141 Lewis Street, Garden Grove—corner of Chapman Avenue and Lewis Street, off the junction of the Santa Ana, Orange, and Garden Grove freeways; (714) 971–4000. Free. Open daily from 9:00 A.M. to 4:30 P.M.; also available are a visitor center, guided tours, and organ recitals. Call ahead for information on attending church services and special events ("The Glory of Christmas," "The Glory of Easter"), or obtaining personal counseling; the weekly televised services and the special events are well attended.

Dr. Robert H. Schuller, founder of the Crystal Cathedral, is known to millions of people through his weekly "Hour of Power" television show and best-selling books like *Move Ahead with Possibility Thinking.* Schuller, a minister of the Reformed Church in America and a protégé of Norman Vincent Peale, began his ministry in Garden Grove by holding weekly services at the Orange Drive-in Theater; he preached from the top of the snack bar while his wife, Arvella, played the organ. By preaching the positive force of Christianity to promote success in daily living, Schuller attracted a growing congregation. In 1970 he went on television and today has the largest audience provided by this electronic medium. Unlike those who have used television to preach religion and create scandal in their personal lives, Schuller and his ministry continue to be widely respected for their integrity and service to people. The recipient of many prestigious awards and honorary degrees, Schuller is a board member of the Orange County chapter of the National Conference of Christians and Jews.

The Crystal Cathedral is an unusual and awe-inspiring house of worship, one worthy of visiting regardless of one's religious faith. Designed by Philip Johnson, this first all-glass church was dedicated in 1980. The cathedral is huge: 415 feet long, 207 feet wide, and 128 feet high. Large panes of glass cover the entire structure of 16,000 steel trusses. The sanctuary seats nearly 3,000 persons on the main floor and in the east, west, and south balconies. Everyone inside can see what the television audience sees, via a giant Sony screen, the first of its kind used for church service. Music is provided by a 14,000-pipe organ, one of the largest in the world and named in honor of Hazel Wright, a church benefactor.

THE WAYFARERS CHAPEL

5755 Palos Verdes Drive, Palos Verdes; (213) 377–1650. Free. Open daily, 11:00 A.M. to 4:00 P.M.

This stunning chapel, national monument to Emanuel Swedenborg, a prominent theologian and philosopher, was designed by Frank Lloyd Wright, one of America's greatest architects. The chapel is built of redwood, glass, and stone and is set on a bluff overlooking the Pacific Ocean. It is surrounded by exquisite gardens.

LOS ANGELES ATTRACTIONS

MORMON TEMPLE
Los Angeles Temple Visitor Center, Church of Jesus Christ of the Latter Day Saints, 10777 Santa Monica Boulevard, Westwood, Los Angeles; (213) 474–5569. Free. Visitor center open daily, 9:00 A.M. to 9:30 P.M.; temple closed to non-Mormons.

The visitor center contains exhibits on the faith and history of the Mormons. Open to all is a genealogical library (the Mormons maintain an extensive and continually growing genealogical collection). Films are shown on the traditional Mormon concept of family life and on strengthening morality for our modern times. The center and temple are situated on ornamented grounds.

5

Greater Los Angeles Outdoor Recreation, Sports, and Entertainment

Whether you want to participate in sports and recreational activities, watch the professionals, or be entertained with music, theatre, and dance, Greater Los Angeles has it all and in abundance.

Sports and Recreational Activities

In addition to the recreational venues listed below, major hotels offer heated swimming pools, spas (Jacuzzis, etc.), and health and fitness facilities (weight and exercise rooms, steam baths, etc.). Even budget-priced hotels at least have a heated swimming pool. Many deluxe hotels can also make arrangements for you to play golf and tennis at public facilities or private clubs.

PACIFIC OCEAN BEACHES

A visit to Greater Los Angeles would not be complete without some time spent on its the broad, sunny beaches, forty-eight of them along 70 miles of coastline, plus many other beaches in Orange County. Don't fret if you forget your bathing suit—there are as many swimsuit shops in Southern California as taco stands, with many selling the latest styles at discounts.

One popular beach in the metropolitan area is Malibu, where the waves break perfectly for surfing (at Malibu Surfrider State

Beach; best surfing August through September) and where many top entertainers and big shots live. Other popular beaches are at Santa Monica, with its famous pier and Palisades Park; Venice Beach, well known for its gorgeous bikini-clad maidens, volleyball enthusiasts, roller skaters, and bodybuilders at the weight-lifting area known as Muscle Beach, as well as for some exceptionally bizarre human beings; Marina del Rey, with the world's largest human-made marina; and the beaches at Manhattan, Hermosa, Redondo, Torrance, San Pedro, Rancho Palos Verdes, Long Beach, and Seal Beach.

In adjacent Orange County, south of Los Angeles County, the beaches are Huntington, Costa Mesa, Newport, and Laguna. There are public parking at and easy access to the beaches. You can get a terrific tan any time of the year, though swimming is best in the summer. Surfers should bring their wet suits.

Other beach-area activities include cruises out on the blue Pacific and to lovely Catalina Island, pier and charter boat fishing, sailboarding, jogging, biking, and just sitting back and enjoying the sparkling ocean and spectacular sunsets. At many of the beaches is a lavish array of restaurants, cafes, shops, attractions, and enter-tainments. For example, Ports O' Call in San Pedro is a charming, New England–style complex of theme and seafood restaurants and unique shops. Fisherman's Village in Marina del Rey re-creates with its shops and restaurants the feel of an old-time seacoast village; it also offers cruises and fishing trips.

OCEAN BOATING AND DEEP-SEA FISHING

Yacht charters; boat, sailboarding, and scuba equipment rentals; harbor and ocean cruises; and deep-sea fishing trips can be arranged in Santa Monica, Marina del Rey, Long Beach, San Pedro, Newport Beach, and other communities along the coast. Providing these services are many companies, such as the Charter Connection (4211 Admiralty Way, Marina del Rey; 213–827–4105) and Widowmaker Sportsfishing Charters (also in Marina del Rey; 213–306–9793).

GOLF

The city of Los Angeles offers seven 18-hole and five 9-hole golf courses; call (213) 485–5555 for playing permits and locations. For information on other Los Angeles County golf courses, call (213) 738–2961. Greater Los Angeles and Orange County have many semiprivate and private golf courses, some of which offer reciprocal privileges to members of golf clubs in other parts of North America.

TENNIS

Many resorts, hotels, and motels throughout Southern California either have their own tennis courts or will assist you in making arrangements to play at nearby facilities. For information on playing at public courts in Los Angeles, call (213) 485–5566.

JOGGING/RUNNING

The best places to jog or run are along the beaches during daylight and in some parks. Better hotels offer jogging maps with designated routes near their locations, or they will recommend safe and pleasurable running areas near them.

BIKING

A superb bike path with runs along beach and ocean stretches from Santa Monica to Torrance, a distance of some 20 miles. Bike-rental facilities are located at Venice Beach and along the beach area of Santa Monica. Bikes are not allowed on freeways, nor should you bike in busy downtown Los Angeles or in unfamiliar areas.

ROLLER-SKATING

If you want to have a truly unique experience, go roller-skating with all the beautiful and strange people at Venice Beach. Roller-skate rentals are available here.

SAILBOARDING AND SAILING

One of the best areas for boat rentals is Marina Beach in Marina del Rey. Equipment rentals are also available at other beaches.

WINTER SKIING

Yes, you can ski in Greater Los Angeles, up in the San Gabriel and San Bernardino mountains that rise in the east. The ski season is from December to April. Ski resorts are located about a two hours' drive from downtown Los Angeles. Weekends are busy times, and the popular places are full to capacity; you are advised to purchase lift tickets in advance by calling these resorts:

Goldmine, San Bernardino Mountains, (714) 585–2519
Mountain High, San Gabriel Mountains, (213) 460–6911
Snow Summit, San Bernardino Mountains, (714) 866–5766
Snow Valley, San Bernardino Mountains, (714) 867–7182

LOS ANGELES RECREATION

The **Big Bear Visitors Bureau** (714–866–5878) will assist you in making reservations and will provide you with information about ski vacation packages, accommodations, restaurants, and snow and driving conditions.

RECREATIONAL PARKS

Not far from downtown Los Angeles and throughout Southern California are many recreational parks and wilderness areas. These scenic places offer hiking, nature study, picnicking, and other forms of recreation. Within California's parks you can get away from the frenetic pace of the city for a while and enjoy the wonderful and unique attractions of nature.

Griffith Park in Hollywood, for example, offers golf, hiking, picnic areas, horseback riding, and panoramic views of the city. Will Rogers State Park, off Sunset Boulevard in the Westside area of Los Angeles, was the estate of the great American humorist and where his favorite sport of polo continues to be played on Sundays; call (213) 454–8212 for information. Also within Greater Los Angeles are Palisades Park, Topanga State Park, Santa Monica Mountains National Recreation Area, and the Angeles National Forest, in which the San Gabriel and San Bernardino mountains are located.

For more information on hiking, camping, hunting, fishing, and other forms of recreation in these and other Southern California parks, contact the following:

California Department of Parks and Recreation
P.O. Box 942896
Sacramento 94296
(916) 445–6477

California Department of Fish and Game
1416 Ninth Street
Sacramento 95814
(916) 445–3531

U.S. Forest Service
Appraiser's Building
630 Sansome Street
San Francisco 94111
(415) 556–0122

LOS ANGELES SPORTS

National Park Service
Western Regional Information Office
Fort Mason, Building 201
San Francisco 94123
(415) 556–4122 or (415) 556–0560

National Park Service Information Center
Santa Monica Mountains National Recreation Area
22900 Ventura Boulevard, Suite 140
Woodland Hills 91364
(818) 888–3440 or (818) 888–3770

California Travel Parks Association
(for private campgrounds and recreational vehicle parks)
P.O. Box 5648
Auburn 95694
(916) 885–1624

PROFESSIONAL SPORTS

Championship teams play in Greater Los Angeles and Orange County. Here are the Dodgers, the Raiders, and the Lakers at the top. And then there are the exciting Angels, the Rams, and the Kings, as well as thrilling UCLA and USC basketball and football games. Pasadena, part of Greater Los Angeles, has the Rose Bowl Game, the number-one collegiate football bowl game in the country. In addition, Los Angeles offers thoroughbred racing and polo matches. Having been the site of two Summer Olympic Games—in 1932 and 1984—and with so many major athletic events taking place here throughout the year, Greater Los Angeles can rightly be called America's Capital of Sport.

The following agencies will book tickets purchased by major credit card over the phone for professional and collegiate sporting events:

Ticketron/Teletron, (213) 410–1062
Al Brooks Theatre Ticket Agency, (213) 626–5863
Murray's Tickets, (213) 234–0123
Union Ticket Agency, (213) 469–5889

Los Angeles Dodgers, six-time World Champions of Baseball (once while they were in Brooklyn and five times as a Los Angeles National League team), play their games at Dodger Stadium. The stadium is located at 1000 Elysian Park Avenue in Los Angeles. Call (213) 224–1500 for home-game schedule and ticket availability.

California Angels, baseball team of the American League, play their games at Anaheim Stadium, 2000 State College Boulevard in Anaheim. Call (714) 634–2000 for home-game schedule and ticket availability.

Los Angeles Rams, of the National Football League, also play their games at Anaheim Stadium, 2000 State College Boulevard in Anaheim. Call (714) 937–6767 for home-game schedule and ticket availability.

Los Angeles Raiders, former World Champions of Professional Football, play their games at the Los Angeles Coliseum. Call (213) 322–3451 for home-game schedule and ticket availability.

Los Angeles Lakers, World Champions of Professional Basketball, play games against the Boston Celtics, their arch rivals, and other National Basketball Association teams at the Forum, 3900 West Manchester Boulevard in Inglewood. Call (213) 673–1300 for home-game schedule and ticket availability.

Los Angeles Kings, of the National Hockey League, now have the potential of winning the Stanley Cup—the world championship of pro hockey—with the acquisition of superstar Wayne Gretzky. You can see The Great Gretzky and his teammates skate during their home games at the Forum, 3900 West Manchester Boulevard in Inglewood. Call (213) 673–1300 for home-game schedule and ticket availability.

Los Angeles Colts Polo Team rides against its competition at the Los Angeles Equestrian and Polo Center, 480 Riverside Drive in Burbank. Call (818) 840–9063 for the home-game schedule and for a schedule of other equestrian events.

THOROUGHBRED RACING
Santa Anita Park, a historic and ornamental thoroughbred race-track, 285 West Huntington Drive, Arcadia; (818) 574–7223

Los Alamitos Race Course, for quarter-horse, harness, and thoroughbred racing, 4961 Katella Avenue, Los Alamitos, near Disneyland; (714) 995–1234

Hollywood Park, called the Track of Lakes and Flowers, for harness and thoroughbred racing, 1050 South Avenue, Inglewood; (213) 677–7151

Catamaran enthusiasts gather on the shoreline.

Entertainment

THEATER AND MUSIC

Not only do Greater Los Angeles and Orange County do a terrific job of entertaining the world through movies and television, but this huge metropolitan region offers every form of entertainment for the folks who live here and for you, the visitor. Symphony, ballet, opera, drama, comedy, jazz, rock and roll—every form of cultural and popular entertainment take place in one or another mix of offerings every day of the year. People who say Los Angeles is a cultural wasteland are either smoking locoweed or too envious to concede that it does have everything. To find out what entertainments are taking place when you are visiting the area, see the *Los Angeles Times, Los Angeles Magazine, Where,* the *Los Angeles Herald Examiner, Reader,* or *L.A. Weekly.* Your hotel concierge or guest relations person is another important source of information on current entertainment offerings and can also be helpful in obtaining tickets.

The following companies will book tickets purchased by major credit card over the phone for the theater, concerts, and other entertainment events:

Ticketron/Teletron, (213) 410–1062
Al Brooks Theatre Ticket Agency, (213) 626–5863
Murray's Tickets, (213) 234–0123
Union Ticket Agency, (213) 469–5889

Music Center, 135 North Grand Avenue, Los Angeles; (213) 972–7211. This modern, wonderful performing arts complex, located in downtown Los Angeles, figures prominently in the city's cultural life. The Music Center consists of three separate theaters: the Dorothy Chandler Pavilion (main concert hall for the Los Angeles Philharmonic orchestra), the Mark Taper Forum, and the Ahmanson Theatre. The Music Center complex also has restaurants, lounges, and underground parking.
Los Angeles Theatre Center, 514 South Spring Street, Los Angeles; (213) 627–5599. Located in the heart of downtown and partly in a former bank building, the center is a complex of several theaters that present established and new plays. There is a cocktail bar here, as well as parking.
Henry Fonda Theatre, 6126 Hollywood Boulevard, Hollywood;

(213) 410–1062. The Henry Fonda is the first theater in Greater Los Angeles to be named after a leading movie and stage star. The theater is a favorite playhouse for dramas and comedies.

Shubert Theatre, 2020 Avenue of the Stars, Century City; (213) 201–1500. The Shubert is the main venue in Greater Los Angeles for top Broadway musicals and other hit shows.

Pantages Theatre, 6233 Hollywood Boulevard, Hollywood; (213) 410–1062. An exceptional example of art deco design, the Pantages Theatre presents musicals, comedies, and dramas.

UCLA Center for the Performing Arts, 10290 Wilshire Boulevard, Westwood; (213) 825–9261. This outstanding performing arts complex consists of four facilities for music, dance, and theater: Royce Hall, Schoenberg Hall, Wadsworth Theatre, and Doolittle Theatre.

Excalibur Theatre, 23305 Mulholland Drive, Woodland Hills; (818) 883–2800. Offered at the Excalibur are Broadway shows, concerts, dramas, and comedies.

Greek Theatre, 2700 North Vermont Avenue, Hollywood; (213) 410–1062. Here you can see such performers as the Gregg Allman Band and the Charlie Daniels Band, as well as special touring groups, such as the Royal National Ballet of Spain.

Hollywood Bowl, 2301 North Highland Avenue, Hollywood; (213) 850–2000. As the favorite outdoor concert place in Greater Los Angeles, the Hollywood Bowl is summer home for the Los Angeles Philharmonic orchestra. In addition, many top performers, such as Andy Williams, sing here. Fireworks displays in the evening sky are also part of the summer entertainment program.

Universal Amphitheater, 100 Universal City Plaza, Universal City; (818) 980–9421. This stage presents top pop performers—Smokey Robinson, Tiffany, and many others.

Variety Arts Center, 940 South Figueroa Street, Los Angeles; (213) 623–9100. A downtown entertainment center offering dancing, comedy, and dinner shows.

DINNER THEATERS

La Cage Aux Folles, 643 North La Cienega Boulevard, West Hollywood; (213) 657–1091, expensive. This restaurant features a rollicking stage show by female impersonators, billing itself as the "most outrageous supper club" in Los Angeles with "all star celebrity impressionists."

Medieval Times, 7662 Beach Boulevard, Buena Park, near Disneyland; (714) 521–4740. Moderate. Medieval Times offers a four-course dinner in a simulated, eleventh-century–style castle, along with a jousting show by costumed knights. The medieval pomp and pageantry include battles on horseback with lances and on the ground with swords and axes.

In The Dark Productions, 2592 Adelbert Avenue, Los Angeles; (213) 661–5777. Expensive. Here you are witness to a murder and help solve the crime. You also get to dine with the actors. Great fun and well worth the price of admission.

COMEDY CLUBS

Comedy and Magic Club, 1018 Hermosa Avenue, Hermosa Beach; (213) 372–1193.

Comedy Store, 8433 Sunset Boulevard, West Hollywood; (213) 656–6225. Do not be surprised to find Robin Williams or Eddie Murphy doing a night's stint here just for laughs.

Groundling Theatre, 7307 Melrose Avenue, Los Angeles; (213) 934–4747. A small theater that puts on hilarious comedy revues. Comics like Pee-wee Herman cut their joke teeth here before becoming top laugh getters.

The Ice House, 24 North Mentor Avenue, Pasadena; (818) 577–1894. The oldest comedy club in Greater Los Angeles.

Igby's Comedy Cabaret, 11637 Tennessee Place, West Los Angeles; (213) 477–3553.

The Improvisation. At several locations in Greater Los Angeles; call (213) 651–2583. Creating laughs for more than a quarter century, which adds up to a lot of terrific and lousy jokes.

L. A. Cabaret Comedy Club, 17271 Ventura Boulevard, Encino; (818) 501–3737. It is not unusual to see top-star comics doing their routines here.

L.A. Connection, 13442 Ventura Boulevard, Sherman Oaks; (818) 784–1868.

Laugh Factory, 8001 Sunset Boulevard, Hollywood; (213) 656–8860.

DANCE PLACES

Annabelle's, 1700 South Pacific Coast Highway, Redondo Beach; (213) 316–1434.

Club Lingerie, 6507 West Sunset Boulevard, Hollywood; (213) 466–8557.

Sash, 11345 Ventura Boulevard, Studio City; (818) 769–5555.

Stock Exchange, 605 South Spring Street, downtown Los Angeles; (213) 627–4400.

LOS ANGELES ENTERTAINMENT

Vertigo, 1024 South Grand Avenue, downtown Los Angeles; (213) 747–4849.

JAZZ PLACES
Alleycat Bistro, 3865 Overland Avenue, Culver City; (213) 204–3660.
At My Place, 1026 Wilshire Boulevard, Santa Monica; (213) 451–8596.
Concerts by the Sea, 100 Fisherman's Wharf, Redondo Beach; (213) 379–4998.
Donte's, 4269 Lankershim Boulevard, North Hollywood; (818) 769–1566.
Hop Singh's, 4110 Lincoln Boulevard, Marina del Rey; (213) 822–4008.
Nucleus Nuance, 7267 Melrose Avenue, Hollywood; (213) 939–8666.
Vine Street Bar and Grill, 1610 North Vine Street, Hollywood; (213) 463–4375.

BARS
Joe Allen, 8706 West Third Street, Los Angeles; (213) 274–7144.
Barney's Beanery, 8447 Santa Monica Boulevard, West Hollywood; (213) 654–2287.
Tom Bergin's, 840 South Fairfax Avenue, Los Angeles; (213) 936–7151.
Casey's Bar and Grill, 613 South Grand Avenue, downtown Los Angeles; (213) 629–2353.
Cat and Fiddle Pub, 6530 Sunset Boulevard, Hollywood; (213) 468–3800.
Grand Avenue Bar. At the Biltmore Hotel, 515 South Grand Avenue, downtown Los Angeles; (213) 624–1011.
Molly Malone's Irish Pub, 575 South Fairfax Avenue, downtown Los Angeles; (213) 935–1577.
Mucky Duck, 1810 Ocean Avenue, Santa Monica; (213) 395–1144.
Polo Lounge. At the Beverly Hills Hotel, 9641 Sunset Boulevard, Beverly Hills; (213) 276–2251. This is one of the top "must be seen in" bars in Greater Los Angeles—an indispensable watering hole for movie stars and billionaires.
Rebecca's, 2025 Pacific Avenue, Venice; (213) 306–6266.

LOS ANGELES ENTERTAINMENT

Simply Blues, 6290 West Sunset Boulevard, Hollywood; (213) 466–5239.

Stepps on the Court. At the Crocker Center, 330 South Hope Street, downtown Los Angeles; (213) 626–0900.

T.G.I. Friday's, 13470 Maxella Avenue, Marina del Rey; (213) 822–9052.

Ye Olde King's Head, 116 Santa Monica Boulevard, Santa Monica; (213) 451–1402.

6

Greater Los Angeles and Orange County Accommodations

There are more than sixty-five thousand hotel rooms in Greater Los Angeles, with hundreds more being added every year. The best hotels in downtown Los Angeles and in the western communities (West Hollywood, Beverly Hills, Century City, Westwood, Bel Air, Santa Monica, Marina del Rey, and those along Wilshire Boulevard) are expensive. A double at these palaces goes for more than $100 a night. There are, of course, many budget places, some of which are listed below. Quality hotels at moderate prices are sorely needed in downtown Los Angeles, but real estate is expensive and developers will continue building to cater to the high end of the market. My own choice would be to stay at a better hotel, where one receives more value, service, amenities, safety, and enjoyment for the money, even though rates are higher. Almost all the deluxe hotels offer special lower rates on weekends and package plans for families; some even offer free stays for children in the same room with parents. Your hometown travel agent will assist you in making the right choices for what you can afford.

The **Southern California Hotel Reservation Center**—call toll-free (800) 537–7666; in California, (800) 527–9997—will help you select, price, and reserve accommodations at resorts, hotels, motels, inns, and bed-and-breakfast places in the areas covered by this guide: Greater Los Angeles, Orange County, Santa Barbara, San Diego, and Palm Springs (the latter three communities are featured in chapters 8 through 10 respectively).

Downtown Los Angeles Hotels

BEST WESTERN DRAGON GATE INN
818 Hill Street; (213) 617–3077 or (800) 528–1234. Moderate.
Located in fascinating Chinatown. Offers a restaurant and other amenities.

BILTMORE HOTEL
506 South Grand Avenue; (213) 624–1011 or (800) 421–8000 (in California, 800–252–0175). Expensive.
The Biltmore is one of the city's great hotels. It has been host to leading movie stars, political figures, and business tycoons. When the Biltmore opened in 1923, it was the largest and best hotel west of Chicago. The concept of the Oscar awards for motion picture excellence was first designed here on a tablecloth in the Crystal Ballroom.

The Biltmore was used as location in several movies—*The Sting, The Poseidon Adventure, Beverly Hills Cop, Ghostbusters,* and *A Star Is Born*—and in the TV series *Hill Street Blues.* This Los Angeles landmark hotel has completed a $40 million renovation.

The European palace–like classical interiors are richly splendid—sumptuously ornate, to be exact—but in the best of taste. Royalty would feel right at home here with all the tasteful extravagance; in fact, Queen Beatrix of the Netherlands and the present Duke and Duchess of York have been guests. Beautiful public rooms are the Gallery Bar, the Cognac Room, the Crystal Ballroom, and the lobby.

The Biltmore is renowned for excellence in personal service. Comfortable, attractively decorated rooms have many nice touches and amenities—for example, Jim Dine engravings. If price is no barrier, staying in the Presidential Suite is like having your own mansion in downtown Los Angeles. The hotel's classic gourmet restaurant is Bernard's. The Court Cafe is for casual dining; the Cognac Room, for sipping rare cognacs and vintage ports; and the Grand Avenue Bar, the place to be for all-star jazz entertainment. Afternoon tea is served in the Rendezvous Court, with its 3-story ceiling of rococo details. The Biltmore has a full-service health club with a swimming pool, various health and fitness devices, a sauna, and massage services. A multilingual staff is on hand for non-English-speaking guests.

76

LOS ANGELES ACCOMMODATIONS

HOLIDAY INN CONVENTION CENTER
1020 South Figueroa Street; (213) 748–1291 or (800) 465–4329. Moderate.

Near Convention Center and close to shopping. Has a restaurant, a lounge, and a swimming pool; provides airport transportation.

HOWARD JOHNSON'S LOS ANGELES CENTRAL
1640 Marengo Street; (213) 223–3841 or (800) 654–2000. Moderate.

A full-service hotel in a central location. Amenities include a restaurant, a lounge, a swimming pool, and shuttle service in a 5-mile radius.

HYATT REGENCY LOS ANGELES
711 South Hope Street; (213) 683–1234 or (800) 228–9000. Expensive.

Located in the Financial District and near the Convention Center, this Hyatt offers excellent accommodations, dining, and lounges, plus health and fitness facilities. Angeles's Flight is a rooftop revolving restaurant for lunch, dinner, and cocktails (moderate to expensive). Pavan is refined but very comfortable, featuring such dishes as sautéed swordfish and lamb tenderloin en croute.

HYATT WILSHIRE
3515 Wilshire Boulevard; (213) 381–7411 or (800) 228–9000. Expensive.

An attractive hotel in a good location. Excellent accommodations, dining, and services. Has a swimming pool, health and fitness facilities, and a baby-sitting service. Cafe Carnival, moderate in price, offers fish, veal, and steaks.

LOS ANGELES HILTON AND TOWERS
930 Wilshire Boulevard; (213) 629–4321 or (800) 445–8667. Expensive.

Downtown location near cultural, shopping, and sports attractions. Offers exceptional accommodations and dining, a swimming pool, and health and fitness facilities. Cardini is a formal dining room that specializes in northern Italian cuisine.

NEW OTANI HOTEL AND GARDEN
120 South Los Angeles Street; (213) 629–1200 or (800) 421–8795. Expensive.

A deluxe hotel located near the Music Center and Little Tokyo. Otani amenities include restaurants, lounges, airport bus service, and a Jacuzzi. There are two levels of shopping in the complex and a lovely Japanese garden. Commodore Perry's, the hotel's gourmet restaurant, offers prime steaks and fresh seafood (expensive). A Thousand Cranes has Western and tatami seating; it overlooks the hotel's tranquil Japanese garden with waterfall and offers traditional Japanese cuisine (expensive).

SHERATON GRAND HOTEL
333 South Figueroa Street; (213) 617–1133 or (800) 325–3535. Expensive.

This is Sheraton's deluxe hotel in the heart of downtown Los Angeles. It offers butler service on every floor, a lounge serving British-afternoon "high tea," a swimming pool, and many other excellent amenities. Ravel is the hotel's acclaimed gourmet restaurant. Live entertainment and dancing are the fare at Tango, and four on-premises movie theaters show the latest films.

SHERATON TOWN HOUSE
2961 Wilshire Boulevard; (213) 382–7171 or (800) 325–3535. Expensive.

Located across from Bullocks Wilshire department store. Fine accommodations and dining, cocktail lounges, a swimming pool, and tennis.

UNIVERSITY HILTON
3540 South Figueroa Street; (213) 748–4141 or (800) 445–8667. Expensive.

This Hilton is near the USC campus and the Coliseum, site of two Summer Olympic Games. Top accommodations and dining, a swimming pool, and other amenities are offered.

WESTIN BONAVENTURE
404 South Figueroa Street; (213) 624—1000 or (800) 228–3000. Expensive.

The Bonaventure is Southern California's futuristic-appearing hotel. No doubt you have seen its cylindrical towers in a number of motion pictures and television shows—*To Live and Die in L. A., Moonlighting, General Hospital.* Located downtown in the heart of the Financial District, the hotel offers comfortable rooms and suites, a stunning atrium lobby, hanging gardens, a garden deck with a swimming pool, and many guest amenities. Bubble elevators shoot up from reflecting pools to guest rooms. Top of Five is its sky-high (35 stories up), revolving restaurant, showing off the panorama of enchanting Los Angeles while you dine and offering American foods, like lobster and beef (expensive). Culinary award–winning Beaudry's, on the main floor, is decorated in golds and browns accented by fresh flowers; this gourmet restaurant's specialties include rack of lamb and roast duckling. The specialties of Singapore Satay Restaurant blend the cuisines of India, China, Malaysia, and Indonesia (moderate).

WILSHIRE TOWERS HOTEL SUITES
3460 West 7th Street; (213) 385–7281 or (800) 422–7281. Moderate.
　　Full kitchen available in every unit. Other amenities include a swimming pool and complimentary parking.

Westside Los Angeles, Hollywood, and Beverly Hills Area Hotels

BEL AGE HOTEL
1020 North San Vincente Boulevard, West Hollywood; (213) 845–1111 or (800) 424–4443. Expensive.
　　Each room in this deluxe hotel is decorated with original art. Superior accommodations, facilities, dining, and services. Amenities include a swimming pool and a baby-sitting service.

BEL-AIR
701 Stone Canyon Road, Westside Los Angeles; (213) 472–1211. Expensive.
　　The Bel-Air was a favorite with the Ford and Rockefeller families and with such stars as Marilyn Monroe, Gregory Peck, Grace Kelly, and Gary Cooper. Located in prestigious Bel-Air, an enclave for the rich and famous, this small hotel (ninety-two rooms, including thirty-three suites) is early Mission style, consisting of 1- and 2-story buildings and bungalows set within extensive lawns and gardens. The dreamy landscaping features red bougainvilleas, azaleas, California sycamores, and a stream that flows into Bel-Air's version of *Swan Lake* on the premises. Rooms have private entrances and walled patios. The effect is that of an exclusive, secluded country inn—a bonus in itself, considering the urban sprawl and frenetic

pace of Greater Los Angeles. The decor of the accommodations is focused on comfort and understated elegance. Guest amenities include a swimming pool, a Zen florist, and a selection of classy automobiles for guest use. The Bel-Air's superb restaurant offers a variety of cuisines: American, Italian, and both French nouvelle and classical French. Highly recommended for those who want the best. A member of Preferred Hotels and Relais Chateaux.

BEVERLY HILLS HOTEL
9641 Sunset Boulevard, Beverly Hills; (213) 276–2251 or (800) 792–7637. Expensive.

The Beverly Hills is one of America's great hotels. Here the stars, movie big shots, writers, directors, and those wanting to make it in the glitz business have congregated for years, like the swallows at Mission San Capistrano. This world-class hotel is surrounded by luxury bungalows on twelve acres of lush grounds. The hotel's Polo Lounge is where multimillion-dollar deals are made and where the stars shine; the Coterie is the place for gourmet dining. Other amenities include a swimming pool and tennis. Highly recommended for those who want excellent quality, and *the* place to soak up the ambience of where star history is made.

BEVERLY HILTON
9876 Wilshire Boulevard, Beverly Hills; (213) 274–7777 or (800) 445–8667. Expensive.

This Hilton, owned by entertainer-tycoon Merv Griffin, is the largest hotel in Beverly Hills and is located near Rodeo Drive. It offers choice accommodations and dining. Amenities include restaurants and lounges, a swimming pool, a health and fitness facility, and airport bus service. L'Escoffier is the hotel's award-winning penthouse restaurant, serving classic French dishes and offering romantic dancing and panoramic views of the city (expensive). The popular Trader Vic's, serving Chinese and Polynesian foods, is also at the Hilton (expensive).

BEVERLY PAVILION HOTEL
9360 Wilshire Boulevard, Beverly Hills; (213) 273–1400 or (800) 421–0545. Expensive.

Superior accommodations and dining in the heart of swank Beverly Hills. Amenities include a swimming pool, restaurants, and a cocktail lounge.

The Japanese community of Little Tokyo offers many fine accommodations, restaurants, and shops. Photo courtesy of
Greater Los Angeles Visitors and Convention Bureau

BEVERLY RODEO HOTEL

360 North Rodeo Drive, Beverly Hills; (213) 273–0300 or (800) 421–0545. Expensive.

Located on ritzy Rodeo Drive, the famous shopping thoroughfare for movie stars and billionaires. First-class accommodations and dining, plus many other guest amenities.

BRENTWOOD SUITES HOTEL

199 North Church Lane; (213) 476–6255. Moderate.

Spacious suites with kitchens. Convenient location near Hollywood area attractions. Offers a swimming pool, continental breakfast, and other services.

DAYS INN CENTURY CITY

10320 West Olympic Boulevard, Century City; (213) 556–2777 or (800) 325-2525. Moderate to expensive.

A new, full-service hotel offering good-value accommodations and amenities, such as a restaurant and a cocktail lounge. Rooms for nonsmokers.

FOUR SEASONS HOTEL LOS ANGELES

300 South Doheny Drive at Burton Way, Westside Los Angeles; (213) 273–2222 or (800) 332–3442. Expensive.

A superb location: in a quiet neighborhood but near Beverly Hills and fashionable Rodeo Drive. The Four Seasons chain operates some of the best luxury hotels in North America, and this one in Los Angeles is in the top rank of accommodations available in the city. The hotel offers restaurants, lounges, a swimming pool, a health and fitness facility, and many other amenities, all of excellent quality. Gardens is a charming, California-style dining room—*the* place to go for Sunday brunch (expensive).

HOLIDAY INN HOLLYWOOD

1755 North Highland Avenue, Hollywood; (213) 462–7181 or (800) 465–4329. Moderate.

Located a short walk from famous Mann's Chinese Theatre. Good accommodations and a revolving restaurant that offers exceptional views of the city, mountains, and ocean. Amenities include a swimming pool and complimentary parking.

HYATT ON SUNSET

8401 Sunset Boulevard, Hollywood; (213) 656–1234 or (800) 228–9000. Expensive.

Overlooks Los Angeles and Hollywood and is near Restaurant Row on La Cienega Boulevard. Splendid accommodations and dining. Has a swimming pool.

J.W. MARRIOTT HOTEL AT CENTURY CITY

2151 Avenue of the Stars, Westside Los Angeles; (213) 201–0440 or (800) 228–9290. Expensive.

This Marriott is the West Coast flagship of the well-known hotel chain. Situated on a 2.7-acre site on the summit of Century City, the hotel has its own exquisitely landscaped garden for the pleasure of guests. Guest rooms, offering wonderful views of the Pacific Ocean or the San Gabriel Mountains, are luxurious, done in muted California tones of tan, peach, and ivory. They feature marble floors and wood moldings, as well as minibars, terry-cloth robes, and hair dryers. The J. W. Marriott has a perfected restaurant, a lounge, twenty-four-hour room service, and complimentary limousine service to nearby attractions.

L'ERMITAGE HOTEL

9291 Burton Way, Beverly Hills; (213) 278–3344 or (800) 424–4443. Expensive.

An aristocratic hotel offering the finest in accommodations, dining, and personal service. Special amenities include limousine service to Beverly Hills locations, fruit and wine in rooms, overnight shoe shines, morning newspapers, and complimentary caviar and pâté during cocktail hours.

MA MAISON SOFITEL

8555 Beverly Boulevard, Westside Los Angeles; (213) 278–5444 or (800) 221–4542. Expensive.

Located five minutes from Rodeo Drive and near the Beverly Center shopping center. Amenities include minibars, twenty-four-hour room service, a swimming pool with a sun deck, a fitness center, a sauna, terraces off some rooms, and complimentary limousine service to shops located in a 5-mile radius. Ma Maison restaurant, the famous place to be seen in, is now within the hotel and serves memorable renditions of French and California cuisines (expensive). Also at this new Los Angeles hotel is La Cajole, a good dining place for breakfast, lunch, and dinner (moderate).

83

MONDRIAN HOTEL

8440 Sunset Boulevard, West Hollywood; (213) 650–8999 or (800) 424–4443. Expensive.

Adapting the design perspective of contemporary artist Mondrian, this top hotel serves modern tastes with quality amenities. It offers restaurants and lounges, a swimming pool, a health and fitness facility, and other services. Cafe Mondrian and Le Terrace have striking views of Los Angeles and serve California nouvelle cuisine (moderate to expensive). There is live jazz in the lounge.

REGENT BEVERLY WILSHIRE HOTEL

9500 Wilshire Boulevard, Beverly Hills; (213) 275–4282 or (800) 545-4000. Expensive.

Newly refurbished to the tune of $65 million, this well-known upscale hotel is located near the glitzy shops and art galleries of Rodeo Drive. It offers superb accommodations, elegant dining, a swimming pool, and many other excellent guest amenities; the level of personal service and guest comfort is first class. Rooms and suites have luxurious furniture, wool rugs, plush marble bathrooms, and acoustical windows to eliminate outside noise. Stewards are available on every floor, and they greet guests on arrival with tea and sliced fruit. Public areas and dining places are richly decorated, the new lobby being more grandiose than the original. The dining room is dignified and serves the finest in classical and contemporary cuisines. A member of Regent Hotels International.

ST. JAMES'S CLUB

8358 Sunset Boulevard, Hollywood; (213) 654–7100 or (800) 225–2637. Expensive.

St. James's Club is a superb art deco landmark in Los Angeles. The air here seems thick with establishmentarian exclusivity. It is a great place to stay if you have "old money," though the nouveau riche are also welcome, and is a favorite with movie stars, directors, and others in the business. Recent renovations cost millions and include special furnishings from Italy. St. James's Club offers excellent accommodations and dining, cocktail lounges, a swimming pool, and a health and fitness facility.

WESTIN CENTURY PLAZA HOTEL

2025 Avenue of the Stars, Westside Los Angeles; (213) 277—2000 or (800) 228–3000. Expensive.

Located within Century City and close to Beverly Hills and Rodeo Drive, the Century Plaza is one of the top luxury hotels in Los Angeles. Its site was once the back lot of Twentieth Century-Fox. Rooms feature private balconies, refrigerator bars, and other niceties. A new tower addition, decorated with fine art and antiques, offers oversize, elegantly furnished rooms and superior amenities. La Chaumiere is the hotel's splendid gourmet restaurant, serving nouvelle California and classic French cuisines; Yamato and the Vineyard are two other excellent restaurants. The grounds have lovely gardens and fountains, as well as a swimming pool. Guests enjoy sports and exercise privileges at exclusive Century West Club. The Century Plaza is one of Ronald Reagan's favorite hotels and has been the choice of presidents since it opened in the mid-1960s.

WESTWOOD MARQUIS HOTEL AND GARDENS
930 Hilgard Avenue, Westside Los Angeles; (213) 208–8765 or (800) 421–2317. Expensive.

World-class luxury accommodations and dining. British-style "high tea" is served in the afternoon. Amenities include exceptionally fine restaurants and comfortable lounges, complimentary limousine service to area shopping and attractions, a swimming pool within a garden setting, and a health and fitness facility. The Dynasty Room, an intimate dining place decorated with Chinese porcelain, serves memorable French and California cuisines (expensive). General Manager Jacques Camus is one of the top hoteliers in Los Angeles, and his philosophy is not complicated: Treat guests like royalty. And a kind of royalty from the business and entertainment world does call the Westwood Marquis their Los Angeles home— Lee Iacocca, Dustin Hoffman, Lauren Bacall, Whitney Houston, and many others.

Universal Studios Area Hotels

COMFORT INN SYLMAR
14955 Roxford Street, Sylmar; (818) 367–0141. Moderate.

Good-value accommodations, a swimming pool, a whirlpool, complimentary continental breakfast, and in-room movies. Near Universal Studios.

MIKADO BEST WESTERN MOTOR HOTEL
12600 Riverside Drive, North Hollywood; (818) 763–9141. Moderate.

Excellent-value accommodations, together with complimentary, full American breakfasts; a swimming pool; a Japanese restaurant; and a lounge. A short drive to Universal Studios and other area attractions.

REGISTRY HOTEL
555 Universal Terrace Parkway, Universal City; (818) 506–2500 or (800) 356–3360. Expensive.
A luxury hotel located next to Universal Studios. It offers good accommodations and dining, cocktail lounges, a swimming pool, and a health and fitness facility.

RESEDA INN
7432 Reseda Boulevard, Reseda; (818) 344–0324. Moderate.
Comfortable accommodations at reasonable prices; some suites with a microwave oven and refrigerator. Offers complimentary continental breakfast, a swimming pool and spa, and rooms for the handicapped.

SAFARI INN
1911 West Olive Avenue, Burbank; (818) 845–8586 or (800) STA–HERE (in California, 800–845–5544). Moderate.
Good-value accommodations, a gourmet restaurant, a swimming pool, and a Jacuzzi; suites with kitchens are also available. Located near area attractions.

SHERATON UNIVERSAL HOTEL
333 Universal Terrace Parkway, Universal City; (818) 980–1212 or (800) 325–3535. Expensive.
This Sheraton is located adjacent to Universal Studios Tour and is 11 miles from downtown Los Angeles; it is also near the new eighteen-theater Cineplex Odeon movie complex. The hotel features an outdoor pool, an exercise room, and a game room. Guest rooms have views of San Fernando Valley, Burbank, or Hollywood Hills. At the top is the Roof Garden Restaurant, and the hotel's live-entertainment nightclub is Comedy Store.

SPORTSMEN'S LODGE HOTEL
12825 Ventura Boulevard, Studio City; (800) 821–1625 (in Canada, 800–341–6363). Moderate.

Good accommodations, a swimming pool, an exercise room, a restaurant, a lounge, and other services. Convenient to area attractions.

Disneyland Area Hotels

All the following deluxe and moderate-rate hotels offer specially priced vacation plans for families and other guests. Work with your hometown travel agent to get the best deal for the right price.

The four roads forming a rectangle around Disneyland and locations for many of the hotels listed below are Harbor Boulevard, Ball Road, Katella Avenue, and West Street. Disneyland's main entrance is on Harbor Boulevard at Freedman Way and near Katella Avenue. All other hotels are on nearby streets or a short drive from the attraction. The main access to Disneyland from Los Angeles is the Santa Ana Freeway South (Interstate 5).

ANAHEIM HILTON AND TOWERS
777 Convention Way, Anaheim; (714) 750–4321 or (800) 445–8667. Expensive.

Deluxe accommodations, a complimentary shuttle to Disneyland, a swimming pool, a recreation deck, and fine restaurants and lounges.

ANAHEIM MARRIOTT HOTEL
700 West Convention Way, Anaheim; (800) 228–9290. Expensive.

Located two blocks from Disneyland. Deluxe accommodations, an excellent French restaurant, a swimming pool, and many other guest amenities.

ANAHEIM PENNY SLEEPER INN
1441 South Manchester Avenue, Anaheim; (714) 991–8100 or (800) 854–6118. Moderate.

Offers queen-size or double beds, a swimming pool, a game room, complimentary transportation to Disneyland, and complimentary continental breakfast.

BEST WESTERN ANAHEIM STARDUST
1057 West Ball Road, Anaheim; (714) 774–7600 or (800) 528–1234. Moderate.

LOS ANGELES ACCOMMODATIONS

Good-value accommodations, a large swimming pool, a restaurant, a lounge with entertainment, and a complimentary shuttle to Disneyland.

BEST WESTERN STOVALL'S INN
1110 West Katella Avenue, Anaheim; (714) 778–1880 or (800) 528–1234. Moderate.
Good-value accommodations. Amenities include a topiary, a whirlpool, and a wading pool.

BUENA PARK HOTEL
7675 Crescent Avenue, Buena Park; (714) 995–1111 or (800) 854–8792 (in California, 800–422–4444; in Canada, 800–325–8734).
An attractive high-rise hotel near Knott's Berry Farm and close to Disneyland. Offers top-quality accommodations, a restaurant, a lounge, a swimming pool, and a nightclub. Family plan available.

CASTLE INN
1734 South Harbor Boulevard, Anaheim; (714) 774–8111. Moderate.
Excellent-value accommodations, offering family and parlor suites, in-room Jacuzzi suites, no-smoking rooms, rooms with refrigerators, complimentary movies and continental breakfasts, and a swimming pool.

CONESTOGA HOTEL
1240 South Walnut Street, Anaheim; (714) 535–0300 or (800) 321–3531 (in California, 800–321–3531; from Canada, call collect, 714–535–2567). Moderate.
Excellent-value accommodations and services. Nicely decorated rooms and suites, complimentary transportation to Disneyland, a swimming pool, a popular restaurant, and a lounge with live entertainment.

DESERT PALM SUITES
631 West Katella Avenue, Anaheim; (714) 535–1133 or (800) 635–5423 (in California, 800–521–6420). Moderate.
A new, 5-story hotel offering spacious rooms and suites, many with balconies; complimentary in-room movies and coffee; an exercise room, sauna, and Jacuzzi; a swimming pool; a game room; and other amenities. Next to Disneyland's south entrance.

LOS ANGELES ACCOMMODATIONS

DISNEYLAND HOTEL
1150 West Cerritos Avenue, Anaheim; (714) 778–6600 or (800) MICKEY–1. Expensive. Note: Because this hotel is in high demand, have your hometown travel agent book accommodations well in advance.

This huge resort complex bills itself as "the official hotel of the Magic Kingdom." It features three high-rise towers of accommodations, sixteen restaurants and lounges, three swimming pools, a tropical beach, and a shopping mall. One of its main attractions is Seaports of the Pacific, an open-air bazaar with waterfalls, waterfront cafes, and complimentary entertainment, such as the popular Dancing Waters show.

EMBASSY SUITES HOTEL
7762 Beach Boulevard, Buena Park; (714) 739–5600 or (800) EMBASSY. Expensive.

An outstanding all-suites hotel. Amenities include a swimming pool, complimentary breakfasts, and complimentary cocktails.

EMERALD OF ANAHEIM
1717 South West Street, Anaheim; (714) 999–0990 or (800) 821–8976. Expensive.

Premium accommodations, a family-style restaurant, a Japanese restaurant, a lounge with live entertainment, and a swimming pool.

HYATT REGENCY ALICANTE
100 Plaza Alicante at Harbor and Chapman in Garden Grove; (714) 971–3000 or (800) 228–9000. Expensive.

Located near Disneyland, the Crystal Cathedral, and other area attractions. A deluxe hotel offering excellent accommodations, dining, and amenities.

JOLLY ROGER INN HOTEL
640 West Katella Avenue, Anaheim; (714) 772–7621 or (800) 854–3184. Moderate.

Excellent-value accommodations located opposite from Disneyland. Offers two swimming pools, a wading pool, a coffee shop, a restaurant, and nightly live entertainment.

QUALITY HOTEL AT CONVENTION CENTER
616 Convention Way, Anaheim; (714) 750–3131 or (800) 228–5151. Moderate.

Excellent-value accommodations located adjacent to the Convention Center and near Disneyland. Good rooms, a swimming pool, a restaurant, a beauty shop, a lounge with entertainment, and a complimentary shuttle to Disneyland.

RAFFLES INN ANAHEIM
2040 South Harbor Road, Anaheim; (714) 750–6100 or (800) 654–0196 (in California, 800–233–6583; in Canada, 800–345–0645).

Excellent-value accommodations. Offers spacious, well-appointed rooms; suites with a minibar and kitchenette; free continental breakfast; a shuttle to Disneyland; and a swimming pool and Jacuzzi.

RAMADA SUITES
1320 South West Street, Anaheim; (714) 776–9246 or (800) 272–6232. Moderate to expensive.

A very nice all-suites hotel, located within walking distance of Disneyland. Offers many amenities, including a swimming pool and spa, a restaurant and cocktail lounge, and complimentary transportation to Disneyland.

SHERATON ANAHEIM HOTEL
1015 West Ball Road, Anaheim; (714) 778–1700 or (800) 325–3535. Expensive.

Located next to Disneyland and the Convention Center. Offers desirable accommodations, prizewinning landscaped grounds, a swimming pool and a game room. Also features a restaurant serving gourmet California cuisine, a New York–style deli, a sushi bar, and a nightclub with entertainment and dancing.

WESTIN SOUTH COAST PLAZA
666 Anton Boulevard, Costa Mesa; (714) 540–2500 or (800) 228–3000. Expensive.

This deluxe hotel is located within a fifteen-minute drive of Disneyland and Knott's Berry Farm and a five- to ten-minute drive to ocean beaches. Nearby are theaters, restaurants, gardens, art galleries, and shopping centers, such as the fabulous South Coast Plaza. The hotel features five restaurants and lounges, a swimming pool, tennis courts, a volleyball court, and a putting green. For the past nine years the hotel's Alfredo's Ristorante has received the gold award of merit in Italian cuisine from the Southern California Restaurant Writers Association; specialties include superb veal and homemade pasta dishes.

Los Angeles Beach Area Hotels

BAY VIEW PLAZA HOLIDAY INN
530 Pico Boulevard, Santa Monica; (213) 399–9344 or (800) 465–4329. Moderate to expensive.
Quality accommodations, including Jacuzzi suites and cabana rooms. Amenities include a restaurant, a lounge, a swimming pool, and a weight room.

BREAKERS MOTEL
1501 Ocean Avenue, Santa Monica; (213) 451–4811 or (800) 634–7333. Moderate to expensive.
Near Santa Monica Pier and Santa Monica Place. Comfortable rooms, a swimming pool, and kitchen units.

HYATT REGENCY LONG BEACH
200 South Pine Street, Long Beach; (213) 491–1234 or (800) 228–9000. Expensive.
This first-class resort hotel features sixteen floors of deluxe accommodations with views of the harbor or coast, a lobby atrium with a lagoon, restaurants and lounges with nightly entertainment, a swimming pool, and many other amenities. The hotel is located near the Convention Center, Shoreline Park, downtown Marina, and Shoreline Village shops and restaurants.

JOLLY ROGER MOTOR HOTEL
2904 Washington Boulevard, Marina del Rey; (213) 822–2904. Moderate.
Good-quality accommodations near Marina del Rey attractions, shopping, dining, and entertainment places. Offers a swimming pool and Jacuzzi.

LITTLE INN ON THE BAY
617 Lido Park Drive, Newport Beach; (714) 673—8800. Moderate to expensive.

LOS ANGELES ACCOMMODATIONS

A nicely located inn, emphasizing traditional New England hospitality and personal service. The Herricks, who own the inn, have created an authentic Cape Cod environment on the seacoast of California. The rooms contain handcrafted, custom-designed replicas of eighteenth- and nineteenth-century furnishings; amenities include continental breakfast and afternoon tea, a swimming pool, bikes, and complimentary boat tours of the bay. You can walk to the beach from the inn.

LOEWS SANTA MONICA BEACH HOTEL
1551 Ocean Avenue, Santa Monica; (213) 458–6700 or (800) 223–0888. Expensive.
A new luxury hotel right on the beach. Excellent rooms and guest amenities, as well as restaurants, cocktail lounges, health and fitness facilities, and a swimming pool.

MALIBU COUNTRY INN
6506 Westward Beach Road, Malibu; (213) 457–9622. Expensive.
All rooms have an ocean view and a patio. Full breakfasts and afternoon cuisine sampling are offered; other amenities include a restaurant, a swimming pool, and a Jacuzzi.

MARINA BEACH HOTEL
4100 Admiralty Way, Marina del Rey; (213) 301–3000 or (800) 882–4000. Expensive.
Luxury rooms and suites, many with views of the Pacific and the world's largest yacht harbor. Stones is the hotel's classic gourmet restaurant, offering such specialties as shrimp in tequila and almond Dover sole (moderate to expensive). Guest amenities include a swimming pool and a lounge.

MARINA DEL REY HOTEL
13534 Bali Way, Marina del Rey; (213) 301–1000 or (800) 882–4000. Expensive.
This top hotel is surrounded by water on three sides, offering great views from many rooms. Amenities include gourmet dining, a swimming pool, and a cocktail lounge.

MARINA DEL REY MARRIOTT
13480 Maxella Avenue, Marina del Rey; (213) 822–8555 or (800) 228–9290. Expensive.

A luxury hotel near Villa Marina and Fisherman's Village shopping and dining areas. Excellent accommodations, restaurants, and cocktail lounges; also has a swimming pool and a health and fitness facility.

MARINA PACIFIC HOTEL AND APARTMENT SUITES
1697 Pacific Avenue, Marina del Rey; (213) 452–1111 (in California, 800–421–8151). Moderate to expensive.
Located near fascinating Venice, with all its colorful human types. Has a restaurant and kitchen units.

MIRAMAR SHERATON
101 Wilshire Boulevard, Santa Monica; (213) 394–3731 or (800) 325–3535. Expensive.
On a bluff overlooking the Pacific, this Sheraton is on the site where J. P. Jones, a silver-mining baron and a founder of Santa Monica, built his mansion, which was later sold to King C. Gillette, inventor of the safety razor. When the property was developed into the Miramar Hotel, it accommodated such personalities as Susan Hayward, John and Jacqueline Kennedy, Eleanor Roosevelt, and Charles Lindbergh. The movie biz discovered Betty Grable here. This renovated, expanded hotel offers a swimming pool, three restaurants, and other guest amenities.

PALOS VERDES INN
1700 South Pacific Coast Highway, Redondo Beach; (213) 316–4211 or (800) 421–9241 (in California 800–352–0385). Moderate to expensive.
A good place of accommodation, located at the foot of exclusive Palos Verdes peninsula and adjacent to the beach. Amenities include a restaurant and lounge, a swimming pool, a Jacuzzi, and other services.

QUEEN MARY HOTEL
Located at the end of Long Beach Freeway, Long Beach; (213) 435–3511 or (800) 421–3732. Expensive.
The world-famous cruise liner *Queen Mary* is one of America's unique hotels. It has 390 staterooms, including 17 suites, and offers all the amenities of a modern hotel. It also has 4 restaurants, 3 lounges, shopping, and services for businesspeople, such as meeting rooms and duplicating and secretarial services. You can tour the

ship and then visit the *Spruce Goose,* Howard Hughes's giant air boat, located next door.

RADISSON PLAZA HOTEL AND GOLF COURSE
1400 Parkview Avenue, Manhattan Beach; (213) 546–7511 or (800) 333–3333. Expensive.

Luxury accommodations, as well as a golf course, a swimming pool, restaurants and lounges, health and fitness facilities, and other amenities.

RITZ CARLTON LAGUNA NIGUEL
33533 Ritz Carlton Drive, Laguna Niguel; (714) 240–2000 or (800) 241–3333. Expensive.

Located off the Pacific Coast Highway, between Los Angeles and San Diego, this Ritz Carlton resort hotel is set on a high bluff overlooking the ocean. The beach here offers guests recreation and tranquility. The hotel has cloistered courtyards, an interior of Italian marble and Chippendale-style furnishings, oil paintings, and English cut crystal chandeliers. Ocean-side rooms are recommended. The hotel offers an eighteen-hole, par 70 Robert Trent Jones II golf course, tennis courts, a fitness center, two swimming pools, a jogging trail, a volleyball court, and an ocean beach. Fishing and yacht charters are arranged for guests. Exceptional dining, plus English-style tea in the afternoons is available at this Ritz.

SHANGRI-LA HOTEL
1301 Ocean Avenue, Santa Monica; (213) 394–2791. Moderate to expensive.

An art deco hotel near the beach and Palisades Park. Nice rooms with kitchens; close to restaurants, shops, and swimming.

SHERATON LONG BEACH
333 East Ocean Boulevard, Long Beach; (213) 436–3000 or (800) 325–3535. Expensive.

A new hotel located across from the downtown convention and entertainment complex and near such attractions as the *Queen Mary,* the *Spruce Goose,* and Pacific beaches. Excellent accommodations, amenities, dining, and entertainment are offered.

SHERATON REDONDO BEACH
300 North Harbor Drive, Redondo Beach; (213) 318–8888 or (800) 325–3535. Expensive.

LOS ANGELES ACCOMMODATIONS

The hotel overlooks the Pacific Ocean and popular King Harbor Marina and is located 7 miles south of LAX and near freeways to major attractions. It features an outdoor pool, an exercise room, a lighted tennis court, and in-room service bars. Coral Cafe serves California cuisine; Splash is the hotel's entertainment place. A good location for enjoying the beaches, scuba diving, fishing, and sailing.

Los Angeles International Airport Hotels

COMPRI HOTEL
1985 East Grand Avenue, El Segundo; (213) 322–0999 or (800) 426–6774 (in California, 800–426–6774). Moderate to expensive.
Good accommodations. Rate includes cooked-to-order breakfasts, night snacks, a swimming pool, and a health and fitness facility. Has a restaurant and lounge.

DAYS INN LAX
5101 Century Boulevard, Inglewood; (213) 673–2311 or (800) 325–2525 (in California, 800–634–7210). Moderate.
Good-value accommodations. Has a restaurant, a lounge, and a swimming pool.

HOLIDAY INN CROWNE PLAZA
5985 Century Boulevard, LAX; (213) 642–7500 or (800) 465–4329. Expensive.
Comfortable rooms and many guest amenities, including a restaurant, a lounge, and a swimming pool.

HYATT AT LOS ANGELES AIRPORT
6225 Century Boulevard, LAX; (213) 670–9000 or (800) 228–9000. Expensive.
Deluxe accommodations, restaurants, and cocktail lounges; a swimming pool; and other amenities.

LOS ANGELES AIRPORT HILTON AND TOWERS
5711 West Century Boulevard, LAX; (213) 410–4000 or (800) 445–8667. Expensive.
Reputed to be the world's largest airport hotel and conference center. Offers attractive rooms and suites, nice landscaping and

gardens, health and fitness facilities, a swimming pool, restaurants and lounges, baby-sitting services, and many other amenities.

LOS ANGELES AIRPORT MARRIOTT
5855 West Century Boulevard, LAX; (213) 641–5700 or (800) 228–9290. Expensive.
Premium accommodations, dining, and other guest services. Has restaurants, lounges, a health and fitness facility, nightly entertainment, a swimming pool, and a Jacuzzi.

SHERATON PLAZA LA REINA
6101 West Century Boulevard, LAX; (213) 642–1111 or (800) 325-3535. Expensive.
The hotel provides airport shuttle service and transportation to the beach, shopping areas, Disneyland, and Knott's Berry Farm. Amenities include a swimming pool, a television sports channel in rooms, a rental-car service, an exercise room, and a hair salon. Le Gourmet and Landry's are its top restaurants; Zeno's is a relaxing cocktail place.

STOUFFER CONCOURSE HOTEL
5400 West Century Boulevard, LAX; (213) 216–5858 or (800) 468–3571. Expensive.
A new luxury hotel offering spacious rooms and top-quality guest amenities, restaurants, lounges, a swimming pool, and a health and fitness facility.

TRADE WINDS "ALL SUITES" HOTEL
4200 West Century Boulevard, Inglewood; (213) 419–0999 or (800) 852–0012 (in California, 800–852–0011). Moderate.
Good-value accommodations. Offers suites, complimentary continental breakfasts, a restaurant, a lounge, a swimming pool, and kitchen units.

Pasadena Hotels

DOUBLETREE HOTEL PLAZA LAS FUENTES
191 North Los Robles Avenue, Pasadena; (818) 792-2727. Expensive.

A new hotel, the largest in Pasadena. Offers superior accommodations and dining, a swimming pool, and many other guest amenities. Top location, near City Hall.

EMBASSY SUITES HOTEL—ARCADIA

211 East Huntington Drive, Arcadia; (818) 445–8525 or (800) EMBASSY. Expensive.

An all-suites hotel. Good-value accommodations, offering complimentary breakfast and cocktails, a swimming pool, and other guest amenities.

HOLIDAY INN PASADENA

303 East Cordova Street, Pasadena; (818) 449–4000 or (800) HOLIDAY. Expensive.

Top-quality accommodations and dining, as well as a lounge, a swimming pool, and tennis courts.

HUNTINGTON SHERATON HOTEL

1401 South Oak Knoll Avenue, Pasadena; (818) 792–0266 or (800) 325–3535. Moderate.

Comfortable accommodations and good dining. The hotel is on beautiful landscaped grounds; its amenities include a swimming pool and a tennis court. Cottages are also available at this property.

PASADENA HILTON

150 South Los Robles Avenue, Pasadena; (818) 577–1000. Expensive.

Offers first-class accommodations and dining, a lounge with live entertainment, a swimming pool, and a health and fitness facility.

7

Greater Los Angeles and Orange County Dining and Shopping

Greater Los Angeles has thousands of restaurants, from swank gourmet places to budget family restaurants to fast-food quickies. French cuisine in its classic and nouvelle modes is fashionable and expensive, but so is new California cooking, which creates unique culinary delights by using the extensive array of fresh ingredients available from the state's farms, orchards, dairies, and fisheries. Restaurants specializing in American food—steaks and roast beef, fresh seafood, chicken, ribs—dominate the restaurant scene in Los Angeles. Hamburger, hot dog, and pizza places—even designer/ gourmet pizza and hamburger emporiums—are everywhere. A wide variety of top-quality restaurants are also in the major shopping malls.

Los Angeles is such a vast mosaic of cultures that you can spend every day of your holiday eating a new ethnic food—Chinese, Russian, Tunisian, Greek, Italian, Japanese, Iranian, British, Jewish, Mexican, and so on. In the ethnic enclaves, such as Little Tokyo and Chinatown, the number of restaurants seems to go on forever. On Olvera Street, in historic downtown, Mexican eateries beckon walkers with savory scents of tacos, enchiladas, and roasting meat.

Some of the city's finest restaurants are in the luxury hotels, offering a choice of several dining places within their buildings. La Cienega Boulevard in Beverly Hills is known as Restaurant Row. And along the coast in Santa Monica, Venice, Malibu, Marina del Rey, Long Beach, and the other oceanfront communities are scores of terrific seafood places. The area around Disneyland also has a bewildering choice of eateries.

The prevailing mode of dining in Los Angeles and throughout Southern California is casual and comfortable, which usually means no jacket and tie for men and whatever women believe looks terrific on them. Some restaurants, however, do require men to wear a jacket and tie and women to appear as if they are emerging from the pages of *Vogue*.

Reservations should be made for dinner; you cannot get in without advance booking at some top restaurants. Many fashionable places also require reservations for lunch and even for breakfast, especially those restaurants where business and movie deals are made. In Los Angeles, as in all major cities, the "in" restaurants are an extension of business offices for many executives.

Top Restaurant Choices

Although the following list contains many top restaurants, its main purpose is to present an overview of the great variety of dining places available in Greater Los Angeles and Orange County. For additional suggestions, obtain dining recommendations from your hotel concierge or guest relations person. *Los Angeles Magazine* and Paul Wallach's *Guide to Restaurants of Los Angeles and Southern California* (Guide Publications, Glendale, California, 1988) are other excellent sources of information on dining well in Greater Los Angeles.

"To live well is to eat well," said some wise person. In Southern California you will have plenty of opportunity to do both.

BEAURIVAGE
26025 Pacific Coast Highway, Malibu; (213) 456–5733. Moderate.

A charming seacoast restaurant where continental-inspired dishes, emphasizing Mediterranean cuisines, are prepared with herbs grown on the property. A specialty is wild boar with lingonberries.

BERNARD'S
At the Biltmore Hotel, 506 South Grand Street, Los Angeles; (213) 612–1580. Expensive.

Bernard's is a leading hotel restaurant that makes edible art out of French cuisine. Fresh seasonal ingredients prevail, and irresistible desserts tempt. Exemplary French and California wines are offered.

BESSIE WALLS
1074 North Tustin Avenue, Anaheim; (714) 630–2812. Moderate.
Fine dining in an early California mansion. Specialties include home-style chicken with dumplings, rack of lamb, veal with Monterey cheeses and Salinas Valley artichokes, and Mexican-style breast of chicken. A good selection of California wines.

CANTER'S FAIRFAX RESTAURANT DELICATESSEN AND BAKERY
419 North Fairfax Avenue, Los Angeles; (213) 651–2030. Moderate.
A long-established Jewish deli where you are served great home-style foods by kind but strong-willed waitresses who act like your mother: "You're not eating enough, dalink!"

CARL'S BARBEQUE
5953 West Pico Boulevard, Los Angeles; (213) 934–0637. Inexpensive.
Chow down here for some of the best barbecued ribs in Los Angeles. The cowboys, real and pretended, in your bunch will smack their lips in delight.

CHAOS
834 South Vermont Avenue, Los Angeles; (213) 384–7307. Moderate.
A full menu of popular and exotic Chinese and Cuban dishes, in addition to steak, chicken, and hamburgers.

CHEZ VOUS
713 East Green Street, Pasadena; (818) 792–4340. Moderate.
Pleasurable dining while in the Pasadena area. The chef's specialties include roast loin of veal and delicious renditions of fresh seafood.

CHASEN'S
9039 Beverly Boulevard, Beverly Hills; (213) 271–2168. Expensive.
Here is where to go if you want to dine amongst actors, agents, writers, and various other movie types. Even former president Ronald Reagan likes Chasen's. The cuisines at this very high priced restaurant are American and continental.

CHEESECAKE FACTORY
4142 Via Marina, Marina del Rey; (213) 306–3344. Inexpensive to moderate.

Honest food like hamburgers and omelets, plus forty kinds of cheesecake. Save your dieting for when you get back home.

CITY RESTAURANT
180 South La Brea, Los Angeles; (213) 938–2155. Moderate.

An extensive repertoire of international and eclectic cuisines are prepared for your fancy at City. It is well known for creative cookery in which basic and exotic ingredients are combined into new dishes. Definitely not your ordinary quiche and veal piccata place.

COLUMBIA BAR AND GRILL
1448 North Gower Street, Hollywood; (213) 461–8800. Moderate to expensive.

Wayne Rogers of television fame—M*A*S*H and other shows—is one of the owners of Columbia, which is well liked by folks in the local entertainment industry. Offers well-prepared American foods.

CRAB SHELL
10 Washington Street, Marina del Rey; (213) 821–8737. Moderate.

The oldest seafood restaurant on this part of the California coast, featuring soft-shell crab, calamari, and huge shrimp. The lounge and patio offer ocean views.

DUKES
8909 Sunset Boulevard, Hollywood; (213) 652–9411. Inexpensive to moderate.

A favorite coffee shop for Hollywood people; the focus is on congeniality. Dukes is a nice place to relax while touring the sights of Hollywood.

EL COLMAO
2328 Pico Boulevard, Los Angeles; (213) 386–6131. Inexpensive.

Delicious Cuban food at budget prices; roast pork with black beans is a specialty.

LOS ANGELES DINING

FISH COMPANY

174 Kinney Street, Santa Monica; (213) 392–8366. Moderate.

The Fish Company is a popular Santa Monica seafood restaurant. There is patio dining, along with an oyster bar.

FIVE CROWNS

3801 East Pacific Coast Highway, Corona del Mar; (714) 760–0331. Moderate to expensive.

A Merry Olde England ambience and great roast beef, plus chicken, fresh seafood, and more.

GINGER MAN RESTAURANT

369 North Bedford Drive, Beverly Hills; (213) 273–7585. Moderate.

Actors Carroll O'Connor (Archie Bunker) and Patrick O'Neal operate this fine restaurant not devoid of blarney. Specialties include fresh pasta, veal, and seafood.

GLADESTONE'S 4 FISH

17300 Pacific Coast Highway, Pacific Palisades; (213) GL4–FISH. Moderate.

This popular seafood restaurant draws crowds for its "All You Can Eat" nights, such as all-you-can-eat shrimp on Mondays or all-you-can-eat king crab legs on Wednesdays.

GORKY'S

536 East Eighth Street, Los Angeles; (213) 627–4060. Inexpensive.

Got a craving for hearty borscht and garlicky kielbasa? This Russian American eatery will satisfy the tummies and souls of Slavophiles and other lovers of ethnic foods.

GULLIVER'S

13181 Mindanao Way, Marina del Rey; (213) 821–8866. Moderate.

The setting is Merry Olde England during the reign of Elizabeth I, and the servers are comely maidens plying you with—what else?—prime roast beef and pudding.

HAMPTON'S

1342 North Highland Avenue, Hollywood; (213) 469–1090. Inexpensive.

Hampton's is to hamburger mavens what cabernet sauvignon is to oenophiles. Also offers a bountiful selection of veggies, fruits, and other goodies for salads.

HANSA HOUSE

1840 South Harbor Boulevard, Anaheim; (714) 750–2411. Inexpensive to moderate.

Do you have a lot of hungry people in your family? Hansa House has an all-you-can-eat Scandinavian smorgasbord that will fill up those seemingly bottomless pits with an amazing array of delicious foods. This is an eatery offering terrific value.

HARD ROCK CAFE

8614 Beverly Boulevard, Los Angeles; (213) 276–7605. Inexpensive.

The Hard Rock Cafe became famous in London, and this spin-off in Los Angeles is also a winner. Gourmet hamburgers, including vegetarian ones, are big sellers, as are mesquite-grilled meats, lime BBQ chicken, and fresh fish dishes. Try their watermelon BBQ sauce. Located at the Beverly Center, a major shopping mall.

JASMINE'S

140 Shoppers Lane, Pasadena; (818) 304–9138. Moderate.

An award-winning Chinese restaurant that specializes in classic Mandarin and Szechwan cuisines.

JOE JOSTS

301 Pine Avenue, Long Beach; (213) 436–9821. Inexpensive.

The setting is 1930s Chicago, and ``Joe's Special'' is Polish sausage on rye with Swiss, pickle, and mustard. Other good eats include pickled eggs, huge schooners of beer, and many different kinds of deli sandwiches. Joe's has been a Long Beach favorite for more than sixty years.

JOHNNY REB'S SOUTHERN SMOKEHOUSE

4663 Long Beach Boulevard, Long Beach; (213) 423–REBS. Moderate.

When you sit down, you get a bowl of peanuts and are encouraged to dump the shells on the floor. Then comes succulent BBQ baby back ribs, pork shoulder smoked over hardwood, seafood gumbo, hush puppies, bourbon steak, and fried chicken. When you are through with all these goodies, dig into Johnny Reb's fantastic pecan pie.

LA GOLONDRINA CAFE AND HISTORIC LANDMARK

17 West Olvera Street, Los Angeles; (213) 628–4349. Inexpensive to moderate.

Los Angeles's striking downtown skyline. Photo courtesy of
Greater Los Angeles Visitors and Convention Bureau

The family that operates this enticing Mexican restaurant has been in business since 1924; moreover, the dining place is in the city's first brick building, constructed in 1855.

LA MAISON DU CAVIAR
268 North Beverly Drive, Beverly Hills; (213) 859–9444. Expensive.
A romantic dining place in exclusive Beverly Hills. French and Russian cuisines, as well as several different kinds of vodka and caviar are offered.

LAWRY'S THE PRIME RIB
55 North La Cienega Boulevard, Beverly Hills; (213) 652–2827. Moderate.
Lawry's is famous for this landmark restaurant and the seasoned salt it produces for the dinner tables of America. The prime roast rib of beef, carved at your table, is the best. The restaurant is also popular for its spinning salad.

LEGENDS OF HOLLYWOOD RESTAURANT
6555 Hollywood Boulevard, Hollywood; (213) 464–7790. Inexpensive.
Located on the Walk of Fame, this New York–style deli serves terrific pastrami, corned beef, and stuffed cabbage—and offers chicken soup to strengthen you for more touring.

L'ERMITAGE
730 La Cienega Boulevard, Beverly Hills; (213) 652–5840. Expensive.
A French restaurant superior in food, wines, ambience, and service, with prices to match. Popular with the well-heeled movie crowd.

L'ORANGERIE
903 North La Cienega Boulevard, Los Angeles; (213) 652–9770. Expensive.
Many gourmets have cited L'Orangerie as the best restaurant in Los Angeles, though in a city that boasts many excellent restaurants, the adjective *best* is at most a relative term. There is no doubt, however, that you will dine exceedingly well—and in a refined environment—on new versions of French cuisine at L'Orangerie and be served by pros.

MANDARIN
430 North Camden Drive, Beverly Hills; (213) 272–0267. Moderate to expensive.

Superb Chinese cuisines served in a distinguished setting. Peking Duck is the specialty of the house.

MOUN OF TUNIS
7554½ Sunset Boulevard, Hollywood; (213) 874–3333. Moderate.

A Tunisian restaurant that offers, among many delicious main courses, lemon chicken with almonds. And for entertainment there is traditional, adrenalin-stirring belly dancing.

OVERLAND STAGE RESTAURANT
1855 South Harbor Boulevard, Anaheim; (714) 750–1811. Moderate.

Wild games dishes, unique chili, prime rib, lobster, and fresh seafood served in an Old West setting.

REX RESTAURANT
2106 West Oceanfront, Newport Beach; (714) 675–2566. Moderate to expensive.

A highly regarded dining place overlooking Newport Beach Pier. Specialties include fresh seafood and pasta, plus homemade desserts. Also here is an oyster bar and grill.

REX-IL RISTORANTE
617 South Olive Street, Los Angeles; (213) 627–2300. Expensive.

This first-class Italian restaurant, located downtown, is well known for its six-course meals. It also offers live music during dining hours and dancing afterward.

ROSALIND'S WEST AFRICAN CUISINE
1941 South La Cienega Boulevard, Los Angeles; (213) 559–8816. Moderate.

Rosalind's is unique in Los Angeles because it offers authentic West African food, which includes mashed yams and ground fish and nuts.

SALT SHAKER FAMILY RESTAURANT
240 South Arroyo Parkway, Pasadena; (818) 796–8388. Inexpensive to moderate.

Known for serving ample breakfasts that would satisfy a lumberjack, plus delicious soups and salads and great desserts.

LOS ANGELES DINING

SEVENTH STREET BISTRO
815 West Seventh Street, Los Angeles; (213) 627–1242. Expensive.
Located in the landmark Fine Arts Building, the Seventh Street Bistro attracts enthusiastic diners for its fresh seafood, foie gras, and terrific desserts.

SEVENTY-TWO MARKET STREET
72 Market Street, Venice; (213) 392–8720. Moderate.
This award-winning restaurant, owned by movie stars Liza Minnelli and Dudley Moore, serves American and nouvelle California cuisines.

SHENANDOAH CAFE
4722 East Second Street, Belmont Shores; (213) 434–3469. Moderate.
Southern cooking, down-home hospitality, and interior decorated like an Old South mansion. Here you can feast on gumbo, fried chicken, Cajun prime beef, and hot apple fritters.

SIR WINSTON'S
At the Queen Mary Hotel, Pier J, Long Beach; (213) 435–3511. Expensive.
Have you ever wanted to dine in high style in one of history's great cruise ships? Here is your chance to do so, in the elegant main dining room of the *Queen Mary*. Jackets and ties are a must for men; dressing fantastic is no less a standard for women. The food is continental and California, there is an extensive selection of wines, and the service and the dining experience are first-rate.

SPAGO
1114 Horn Avenue, West Hollywood; (213) 652–4025. Expensive.
At Spago's you can dine on delicious contrasts—for example, lobster ravioli or pizza with duck sausage.

TAM O'SHANTER INN
2980 Los Feliz Boulevard, Los Angeles; (213) 664–4024. Moderate.
This is said to be the city's oldest restaurant under original ownership in the same location. The Tam has a Scottish decor and features prime beef, lamb shanks, and fresh seafood. Sandwiches and ale are served at the bar.

TAYLOR'S PRIME STEAKS
3361 West Eighth Street, Los Angeles; (213) 382–8449. Moderate.
Here is a very good restaurant where you can dine on excellent beef and seafood without fracturing your budget. Be sure to start your meal with Taylor's clam chowder.

TOMMY LASORDA'S RIBS AND PASTA
14130 Marquesas Way, Marina del Rey; (213) 827–5330. Moderate.
Tommy Lasorda not only manages the world champion Los Angeles Dodgers but also owns this popular seacoast restaurant. After you have seen the Dodgers win a home game, come here to celebrate with beef, pasta, and seafood.

THE TOWER RESTAURANT
1150 South Olive Street, at the top of the Transamerica Center in downtown Los Angeles; (213) 746–1554. Expensive.
Superb dining with a panoramic view of the city. The restaurant has an excellent reputation for French cuisine and meticulous service. Specialties include veal chop morel, fresh seafood, and rack of lamb.

WERNER'S
1001 West Lincoln Avenue, Anaheim; (714) 535–5505. Inexpensive.
Treat the family to some terrific home cooking—not yours but Werner's. Finish your meal of ribs, chicken, or whatever with pies like Mama used to make, that is, if she ever made them this good.

THE WINDSOR
3198 West Seventh Street, Los Angeles; (213) 382–1261. Expensive.
An outstanding French restaurant—food, service, dining environment—that has set the standard for elegance and decorum in Los Angeles since the 1940s.

YAMASHIRO
1999 North Sycamore Avenue, Hollywood; (213) 466–5125. Moderate to expensive.
Located high in the Hollywood Hills, Yamashiro is an excellent Japanese restaurant, one of the best in the city. Its architecture and interior are like that of a royal abode. The views of Los Angeles, spreading out below, are spectacular, especially at night, when the city becomes a scattering of brilliant jewels. Traditional Japanese foods are served with elegant grace.

Famous and Fascinating Shopping Areas

There are thousands of stores in Greater Los Angeles and Orange County. Listed below are fabulous shopping centers that offer large department stores and a vast array of specialty shops, restaurants, cafes, cinemas, and services; also listed are old-fashioned food markets and charming theme shopping, dining, and recreational complexes, such as Ports O'Call and Fisherman's Village. If you have a specific need for a product or service, ask your hotel concierge or guest relations person for suggestions. Some hotels will arrange for others to do the shopping for you. In addition, many deluxe hotels, such as the Westin Bonaventure, have shopping galleries of their own.

ALPINE VILLAGE
883 West Torrance Boulevard, Torrance; (213) 327–4384. Open daily from 11:00 A.M.; shops open until 7:00 P.M.
Alpine Village re-creates a Bavarian mountain hamlet in Southern California. This attraction is a colorful shopping area offering quality goods from Europe; it also has a good German restaurant.

BEVERLY CENTER
8500 Beverly Boulevard, Los Angeles; (213) 854-0070.
The city's largest building of shops, department stores, restaurants, and services.

BONAVENTURE SHOPPING GALLERY
404 South Figueroa Street in downtown Los Angeles.
Six levels of shops and restaurants, located within the futuristic Westin Bonaventure Hotel complex.

CENTURY CITY SHOPPING CENTER AND MARKETPLACE
10250 Santa Monica Boulevard, West Los Angeles; (213) 553–5300.
This popular shopping center is located on what was once the back lot of Twentieth Century-Fox film studios. Now the site contains more than 150 stores of all kinds, plus Bullock's department store. The Festival Marketplace has a wide variety of restaurants and cafes, a European-style deli, and vendors offering gourmet foods from around the world. An AMC Century fourteen-theater complex allows you to rest from the shopping and catch up on all the latest movies.

110

LOS ANGELES SHOPPING

You get three hours of complimentary parking by having your ticket validated at stores, services, restaurants, or theaters.

FARMERS MARKET AND SHOPPING VILLAGE
6333 West Third Street, Los Angeles; (213) 933–9211. Free access. Open daily.

In densely populated, urban, fast-paced Los Angeles, it is easy to forget that California is an important agricultural state, producing an immense variety of fruits, vegetables, meats, seafood, and other food products. When you come into Farmers Market you are enveloped in all of California's riches grown on its lands and harvested from its waters. The food vendors here also sell good things to eat from other countries. And cafes here allow you to sit a spell while you drink coffee and munch on something delicious.

FISHERMAN'S VILLAGE
13763 Fiji Way, Marina del Rey; (213) 823–5411. Free access. Open daily 10:00 A.M. to 9:00 P.M.

Fisherman's Village overlooks one of America's largest yacht harbors. At this picturesque complex, you can shop in an assortment of stores, dine in restaurants on fresh seafood from the Pacific, charter a yacht, take a dinner cruise, or go fishing for the day.

KING HARBOR
Located at Redondo Beach; (213) 372–8536. Free access. Open daily.

This waterfront complex has shops, restaurants, hotels, marinas, charter boats for cruises and deep-sea fishing, and various other ocean sports services.

PORTS O'CALL VILLAGE
Located at the end of the Harbor Freeway in San Pedro; (213) 831–0287. Free access. Open daily.

Ports O'Call is a little bit of a New England seacoast village in California. It features seventy-five interesting shops, several restaurants, harbor tours, sailing charters, dinner cruises, and helicopter rides.

RODEO DRIVE
What makes Rodeo Drive unique is its widespread image of exclusivity and conspicuous consumption in the heart of one of the world's wealthiest communities. If you have money to burn, the

merchants of Rodeo Drive welcome you with open arms—or possibly stiff-nosed arrogance. If your bank or credit card balance is woeful, come and window-shop along Rodeo Drive for the fun of it and to tell the folks back home you were here. Some of the choicest stores are Louis Vuitton luggage, Bally of Switzerland shoes, Vidal Sassoon hairstyling, Fred Joaillier jewelry, Gucci clothing and leather goods, Hermes boutique, Hammacher-Schlemmer odds and ends, Giorgio fashions, Tiffany's jewelry, Polo/Ralph Lauren clothing, Elizabeth Arden beauty treatments, Bijan clothing, Cartier jewelry, Yves St. Laurent Rive Gauche fashions, Sotheby's fine art auctioneers, and Van Cleef and Arpels jewelry. The Beverly Rodeo Hotel and the Beverly Wilshire Hotel are also here. Rodeo Drive runs between and at right angles to Wilshire and Santa Monica boulevards in Beverly Hills.

SANTA MONICA PIER
Located at Ocean and Colorado avenues, Santa Monica; (213) 458–8900. Free access. Open daily.

This famous pier has restaurants, shops, a historic carousel, cafes, and bars, as well as places from which to fish and to view the sun setting below the ocean horizon.

SANTA MONICA PLACE
Located between Second and Fourth streets, Colorado, and Broadway in Santa Monica; (213) 394–5451.

Large department stores and 160 specialty shops and restaurants.

SEVENTH MARKET PLACE AT CITICORP PLAZA
725 South Figueroa Street in downtown Los Angeles; (213) 955-7190.

Sixty-five specialty stores, in addition to Bullock's and May Company department stores; a three-level festival marketplace; and many restaurants and cafes.

SHORELINE VILLAGE
407 Shoreline Village Drive, Long Beach; (213) 435–5911.

This charming seaside shopping and dining complex is built on the site of "The Pike," known in the past as the Coney Island of the West, and it still has an operating, original Loof carousel. More than thirty turn-of-the-century theme shops and restaurants are in this complex, which is near the *Queen Mary* and *Spruce Goose* attractions and many area hotels and is next to the Long Beach Convention Center. Shoreline Village is a nice place to come just for a stroll, day or evening.

SOUTH COAST PLAZA
Off the San Diego Freeway in Costa Mesa, near Disneyland and Knott's Berry Farm. Call (714) 241-1700 for more information on shops, restaurants, and special events.

If you have longed to experience a super-duper California shopping mall, South Coast Plaza will make your dreams come true. Its dazzling interior has glittering shopping courts called Carousel, Jewel, and Crystal. The environment is one of garden boulevards decorated with cozy sidewalk cafes, living trees, colorful flowers, and fancy fountains. It is a pleasure just to stroll and window-shop.

Each year, more than 18 million people visit South Coast Plaza, making it a major tourist attraction. Here you can buy just about everything from Mickey Mouse watches to jewels worth thousands of dollars. The plaza contains three hundred stores, including eight major department stores, and thirty restaurants. Also within the plaza are Orange County's magnificent Performing Arts Center, which houses Segerstrom Hall; the South Coast Repertory Theatre; and California Scenario, a 1.6-acre sculpture garden with works by Noguchi, Miró, Calder, Moore, and Dubuffet.

South Coast Plaza has many of the best stores—among them Nordstrom department store, Orrefors crystal, Talbots casual and classic wear for women, Alfred Sung's boutique of understated elegance, Nautica outdoor wear, Scribner's Book Store, American Eagle Outfitters, Overland Trading leathergoods, Esprit, Saks Fifth Avenue, I. Magnin, the House of Almonds, Ralph Lauren, Bally of Switzerland, Benetton, Bruno Magli Italian handbags and shoes, Cartier, Gucci, Ann Taylor, Abercrombie and Fitch, the Banana Republic, Church's English Shoes, Brookstone, British Khaki, F. A. O. Schwarz toys, Laura Ashley, Louis Vuitton, Mark Cross, Rizzoli books, and Eddie Bauer.

THE WEST SIDE PAVILION
On Pico Boulevard in West Los Angeles; (213) 450-1757.

Features some 150 shops, as well as Nordstrom and May Company department stores, and cinemas.

8

Santa Catalina Island and Santa Barbara

Santa Catalina Island

Beautiful Santa Catalina Island lies 22 miles off the coast of Long Beach. On the island the lovely beachfront resort town of Avalon offers visitors sandy beaches and a boardwalk with shops and restaurants. Boats, bikes, tackle, diving equipment, and other recreational gear are available for rent; the Avalon area also has golf, tennis, and sailing facilities.

Imaginative visitors have compared Avalon with the picturesque villages along Italy's Amalfi coast. Attractions include the historic Casino Building, with its famous Avalon Ballroom, still used for big band dancing; the Wrigley Memorial Botanical Garden, exhibiting and preserving the plants of California's islands; and the Descano Beach Club, offering beach and recreational facilities. Motor-coach tours of the island and boat cruises are offered by Catalina Sightseeing Tours (213–510–-2000).

For close to a hundred years this 76-square-mile Shangri-la out at sea has provided Greater Los Angeles and Orange County residents and their visitors with a special island escape. Discovered by explorer Juan Cabrillo in 1542, Catalina Island first became a popular Southern California vacation place in 1892. That year the Banning brothers bought the island and built the Hotel Metropole. In 1919 William Wrigley, the king of chewing gum, purchased the island for $3.5 million, an amount that today might possibly purchase a small bungalow in Beverly Hills. Wrigley constructed his grand summer mansion here, brought his Chicago Cubs on the island for spring training, and built Avalon's famous circular Casino Building. The Avalon Ballroom in the Casino rocked to the big bands of Woody Herman, Jimmy Dorsey, and Harry James. Today the big band sound still plays for dancers. In addition to the ballroom, the

Casino houses an art gallery, a museum, and a movie theater. In the 1920s Zane Grey filmed his epic movie *The Vanishing American* on Catalina; the offspring from the buffalo brought on the island for Grey's film now roam freely in remote areas.

If you have a day or two extra, you will find a visit to Santa Catalina a very pleasant part of your Southern California holiday.

On the island are more than thirty-five hotels, motels, and inns, including the Wrigley mansion, which now serves visitors as a bed-and-breakfast establishment. Recommended places of accommodation include the **Catalina Canyon Hotel** (213–510–0325, moderate), the **Hotel Catalina** (213–510–0027; moderate), the **Hotel St. Lauren** (213–510–2299; moderate to expensive), the **Inn on Mount Ida** (the old Wrigley Mansion; 213–510–2030; expensive), the **"Old" Turner Inn B&B** (213–510–2236; moderate), **Seaport Village Inn** (213–510–0344; moderate), and the **Zane Grey Pueblo Hotel** (213–510–0966; moderate). Recommended restaurants are **Cafe Prego** (213–510–1218; moderate), serving satisfying seafood and Italian dishes, and **The Upstairs Place** (213–510–0333; moderate), offering fresh seafood, steak, and chicken.

Catalina's busiest season runs from Easter week through October, and advance reservations for overnight accommodations are essential. For more information on accommodations, dining, and recreation on the island, call the **Catalina Island Chamber of Commerce** at (213) 510–1520 or the **Long Beach Area Convention and Visitors Council** at (213) 436–3645.

HOW TO GET THERE

From Long Beach and San Pedro, take Catalina Cruises (213–514–3838); from San Pedro, take Catalina Express (213–519–1212), which has a new hydrofoil service and seasonal service from Redondo Beach. Crossing time is less than two hours. Vessels operate throughout the year and provide service to the towns of Avalon and Two Harbors.

Oxnard

Oxnard is a lovely seacoast resort community located between Malibu and Santa Barbara. It offers uncrowded beaches, golf, tennis, sailing and fishing charters, and cruises to Channel Islands National Park. Other attractions include the Carnegie Cultural Arts

Center and the Seabee Museum. Special events held annually are the California Strawberry Festival and the Point Mugu Air Show.

Recommended accommodations are **Casa Sirena** (3605 Peninsula Road; 805–985–6311; expensive), the **Embassy Suites Mandalay Beach Resort** (2101 Mandalay Beach Road; 805–984–2500; expensive), and the **Radisson Suite Hotel** (2101 West Vineyard; 805–988–0130; expensive), which is adjacent to a championship golf course.

For more information on Oxnard attractions and accommodations, write the **Oxnard Convention and Visitors Bureau** at 400 Esplanade Drive, Suite 100, Oxnard 93030, or call (805) 485–8833.

Santa Barbara

Located a mere 90 miles north of the hustle and bustle of Los Angeles is Santa Barbara, a beautiful seacoast city of Spanish colonial charm and lush gardens. Santa Barbara is set like a shimmering orange-topped jewel between the blue Pacific and the tan and olive Santa Ynez Mountains. Santa Barbara was founded in 1782 by Franciscan missionaries from Spain and Mexico. The Mission of Santa Barbara they built here was tenth in a necklace of twenty-one missions along the length of California. Mission Santa Barbara is called the Queen of Missions because of its architectural beauty and historic importance.

HOW TO GET THERE

Santa Barbara is located 90 miles north of Los Angeles, via the Pacific Coast Highway, about a two-hour drive. This is a very scenic drive, with the Pacific Ocean on one side and the mountains on the other, and you go through lovely communities, such as Malibu and Oxnard.

Santa Barbara is linked to Los Angeles Airport (LAX) by commuter airlines and to other key cities by major airlines like United and American. Santa Barbara Airport (805–967–5608) is located 8 miles north of downtown. Rental cars are available at the airport and at downtown locations.

Amtrak provides daily service to Santa Barbara from San Francisco, Los Angeles, and San Diego; call (805) 687–6848.

Greyhound (805–966–3962) has daily service to Santa Barbara from major cities.

SANTA BARBARA

Santa Barbara Airbus (805–964–7759) provides bus transportation to and from LAX and makes eighteen trips daily.

HOW TO GET AROUND

Downtown Santa Barbara is perfect for walking tours, with its sun-washed streets, Spanish colonial architecture, palm trees, and plantings of flowers. State, Anacapa, and Santa Barbara are the main streets of downtown; they run parallel to one another, with Victoria Street at the east end and Ortega Street on the west end of this section. Within this rectangle of downtown streets are the Museum of Art, the library, City Hall, El Presidio, the Historical Society Museum, adobe dwellings, shopping arcades, restaurants, and cafes. The beach and Stearns Wharf are located 7 blocks south from Ortega Street. Mission Santa Barbara is 10 blocks northeast of Victoria Street.

The Santa Barbara Trolley (805–962–0209) will take you to many local attractions, shopping and dining areas, and hotels. Free shuttle bus service operates on State Street every ten minutes, Monday through Friday, 10:00 A.M. to 4:00 P.M.

Santa Barbara Metropolitan Transit District (805–683–3702) provides bus service between the city and the communities of Goleta and Carpinteria.

Taxi, limousine, and rental-car services are also available in Santa Barbara.

Sightseeing services include Courthouse Tours (805–962–6464), Dee's Deluxe Tours (805–966–6268), On the Go (805–965–1408), Sailing Center (805–962–2826), Santa Barbara Trolley Company (805–962–0209), Touring Taxi of Santa Barbara (805–962–2344), and Walking Tours through History (805–967–9869).

TOURISM INFORMATION

For assistance in making your stay more enjoyable, visit the **Santa Barbara Visitor Information Center,** located at Santa Barbara Street at Cabrillo Boulevard, near Stearns Wharf (805–965–3021).

For a free *Official Destination Guide,* write the **Santa Barbara Conference and Visitors Bureau** at 222 East Anapamu Street, Santa Barbara 93101, or call (805) 966–9222.

IMPORTANT TELEPHONE NUMBERS

Police, Fire, Sheriff, Highway Patrol, Paramedics, Mental Health, Dial 911

Missing Children Hotline, (800) 222–3463
Los Angeles Poison Control, (213) 484–5151
Community Assistance Listening Line, (805) 569–2255
Coast Guard Search and Rescue, (805) 569–2255
Santa Barbara Cottage Hospital, (805) 569–7210
St. Francis Hospital, (805) 962–7661
Goleta Valley Community Hospital, (805) 967–3411

Santa Barbara Sports and Recreational Activities

An excellent reason to come to Santa Barbara is for its warm sandy beaches, decorated at their edges with tall swaying palm trees and the blue waters of the Pacific. This is the ideal place for saltwater swimming, sailboarding, sunbathing, and strolling the cares of life away. The area's beaches include Arroyo Burro Beach at Cliff Drive, Butterfly Beach in Montecito, Carpinteria City Beach at Linden Lane, East Beach on Cabrillo Boulevard, Goleta Beach on Sandspit Road in Goleta, Isla Vista Beach at Del Playa Drive, Leadbetter Beach on Shoreline Drive, Rincon Beach on Bates Road in Carpinteria, Thousand Steps Beach at the end of Mesa Lane, and West Beach on Cabrillo Boulevard.

BIKING
Beach Rentals, 8 West Cabrillo Boulevard, across from Stearns Wharf, Santa Barbara; (805) 963–2524
Bike 'n Hike, Coast Village Road, Montecito; (805) 969–0179
Open Air Bicycles, 224 Chapala Street, Santa Barbara; (805) 963–3717
Pacific Traveler's Supply, 529 State Street, Santa Barbara; (805) 963–4438

FISHING, BOATING, CRUISES TO CHANNEL ISLANDS, AND WHALE WATCHING
Captain Dan's Charters, 326 Mellifont Avenue, Santa Barbara; (805) 962–4871
Captain Dave's Channel Island Charter, harbor front area, Santa Barbara; (805) 647–3161
Captain Don's Harbor Tours, ticket booth next to Stearns Wharf, Santa Barbara; (805) 969–5217

Museum of Natural Science Island Cruises, harbor front area, Santa Barbara; (805) 682–4711

Navigator Channel Island Cruise, 1621 Posilipo Lane, Santa Barbara; (805) 969–2393

Santa Barbara Boat Rentals/Sailing Association, at the Breakwater, Santa Barbara; (805) 962–2826

Sea Landing Aquatic Center, at the Breakwater, Santa Barbara; (805) 963–3546

Zuma Charters, at the Breakwater, Santa Barbara; (805) 965–2267

GOLF

Sandpiper Golf Course, 7925 Hollister Avenue, Goleta; (805) 968-1541; eighteen holes

Santa Barbara Community Golf Course, Los Positas Road and McCaw Avenue, Santa Barbara; (805) 687–7087; eighteen holes

HANG GLIDING

Hang Glider Emporium, 613 North Milpas, Santa Barbara; (805) 965–3733

HIKING

Hiking is available on trails in the Santa Ynez Mountains. Maps and information can be obtained from the headquarters of the Los Padres National Forest, at 42 Aero Camino in Goleta. Books and maps on hiking in the Santa Barbara area can be purchased from area bookstores. Information on Sierra Club hikes is available by calling (805) 965–8709.

HORSEBACK RIDING AND POLO

Branchwater Ranches Riding Stables, Lake Cachuma; (805) 688–4658

Circle Bar B Ranch, 100 Refugio Road, Goleta; (805) 968–3901

Gene O'Hagen Stables, 1900 Refugio Road, Goleta; (805) 969–5929

Philip's Horse Rentals, 2190 Banner Road, Summerland; (805) 969–7606

Santa Barbara Polo Club, Santa Claus Lane off Highway 101, Carpinteria; Sunday matches, March through October, 1:00 to 3:00 P.M.

Old Mission Santa Barbara is considered the most splendid in the chain of twenty-one California missions.

HOT AIR BALLOONING
Solvang Balloon Company, 475 First Street, Solvang; (805) 688–7878

ROLLER-SKATING
Beach Rentals, 8 West Cabrillo Road, Santa Barbara; (805) 963–2524

SCUBA DIVING
Diver's Den, 22 Anacapa Street, Santa Barbara; (805) 963–8917

TENNIS
Use permits for public courts are obtained at the Recreation Department, located at 820 Laguna Street in Santa Barbara (805–564–5418).
Las Positas Municipal Courts, 1002 Las Positas Road, Santa Barbara
Municipal Court, 1414 Park Place, Santa Barbara
Pershing Park Courts, Cabrillo Boulevard and Castillo Street, Santa Barbara

SAILBOARDING
Mountain Air Sports, 14 State Street, Santa Barbara; (805) 962–0049
Sundance Windsurfing, 2026 Cliff Drive, Santa Barbara; (805) 966–2474
Windance, 6 West Anapamu Street, Santa Barbara; (805) 962–4774

Santa Barbara Special Events

For additional information on these special events, call the **Santa Barbara Conference and Visitors Bureau** at (805) 966–9222.

WINTER EVENTS
Celebrity Golf Tournament, February
Compadres del los Gatos (all-breed cat show), February
International Film Festival, March
International Cymbidium Orchid Show, March

SPRING EVENTS
Santa Barbara Arts Council Festival, April
Santa Barbara County Vintners' Festival, April
Multicultural Fair, May

SUMMER EVENTS
Summer Solstice Parade, June
Semana Nautica (multisports festival), June
Santa Barbara Kennel Club Dog Show, July
Channel City Kennel Club Dog Show, July
Santa Barbara National Horse and Flower Show, July
Greek Festival, August
Old Spanish Days Fiesta, August
Pacific Coast Open Polo Tournament, August

AUTUMN EVENTS
Santa Barbara Concours d'Elegance (antique and classic car
     show), September
Danish Days (in Solvang), September
Oktoberfest (Munich-style festival), October
Sandcastle and Sculpting Contest, October
Goleta Valley Days, October
Santa Barbara National Amateur Horse Show, November
Yuletide Boat Parade, December

Santa Barbara Attractions

In addition to the attractions listed below, your tour of Santa Barbara
should include Casa del la Guerra, built in 1827 as the home of
Spanish commandante Jose del la Guerra. This was the center of
social life in upper (Alta) California. Santa Barbara's historic adobe
houses include Hill Carrillo Adobe on East Carrillo Street; Orena
Adobes, dated 1848–58; Lugo Adobe on East De La Guerra Street;
Rochin Adobe on Santa Barbara Street; and Santiago de la Guerra,
built in 1812 and one of the oldest dwellings in the city, on East De
La Guerra Street. Mission Santa Barbara, known as the Queen of
Missions, was established in 1786 and continues today as an active
parish church. You can find the Queen of Missions on Mission Canyon Road near the Museum of Natural Science.
     See the Dolphin Fountain—located near Stearns Wharf—which
was sponsored as a Santa Barbara–Puerto Vallarta (Mexico) sister

SANTA BARBARA

city project. Stearns Wharf, built in 1872, offers a setting in which to stroll among gift shops, fresh fish stands, restaurants, and cafes. Here also is Sea Center, a branch of the Museum of Natural History.

Visit Andree Clark Bird Refuge on Cabrillo Boulevard; El Paseo, a street of colonial-style shops, art galleries, and cafes; Hope Ranch, a swank residential area of magnificent homes on beautifully landscaped grounds; and the Nature Conservancy at Stearns Wharf, which has a visitor center and is developing Santa Cruz Island (one of the Channel Islands) into an important nature preserve.

While in Santa Barbara on a Saturday morning, take in the sights and tastes at Farmer's Market, where fresh fruits, vegetables, flowers, nuts, and honey are brought in from country farms. Plaza De La Guerra is the heart of old and new Santa Barbara. Here in 1850 the city council first met. In this area, too, is one of Santa Barbara's first parks; the city is famous for its lovely parks and promenades. Here, too, is City Hall, a fine example of Spanish colonial revival architecture, and the *Santa Barbara News-Press,* Southern California's oldest daily newspaper. Each August, Fiesta Week takes place throughout the city and in the plaza, which is transformed into a colorful bazaar of crafts and food for sale, music, and merriment. The buildings lining State Street—Santa Barbara's main street—were rebuilt in Spanish Colonial design following an earthquake in 1925. On State Street are many shops and a pleasant strolling environment enhanced by beautiful landscaping and benches for relaxation.

The University of California at Santa Barbara invites you to tour its lovely campus. A main landmark is Storke Tower, which has an impressive carillon. Various lectures, concerts, films, and other events are open to the public.

At Santa Barbara's Yacht Harbor and Marina, located at West Cabrillo Boulevard, you can go out on charter fishing boats and whale-watching trips to see the California gray whale. The whales migrate from the Arctic to Mexico from late November through January. After feeding and breeding in warm waters, they head north again during the months of February, March, and April.

The image of Santa Barbara would surely suffer if polo, the sport of the rich, were not played here. Every Sunday from April through October polo matches are played at the Santa Barbara Polo and Racquet Club. Visitors are welcome to attend the matches and picnic on the grounds. Off Highway 101 is Santa Claus Lane, a popular tourist attraction exemplifying roadside vernacular architecture dating from the 1950s. This retailing center contains shops selling toys, candy, dried fruit, baked goods, date shakes, and

124

crystals. A Santa Claus postmark is stamped on mail sent from this attraction.

Montecito ("little forest"), located east of downtown Santa Barbara, is an exclusive residential community that since the late 1800s has attracted millionaires and movie stars, along with artists and writers. The San Ysidro Ranch, Montecito Inn, and Four Seasons Biltmore are places of accommodation frequented by famous personalities and by the press corps that followed former president Reagan. The beautiful Spanish colonial Church of Our Lady of Montecito is also within this enclave of affluence.

Santa Barbara Parks

Santa Barbara is a city of lovely parks. Following are some special ones.

Alameda Park, Santa Barbara Street, located downtown—more than seventy species of trees, as well as picnic areas and a gazebo used for concerts.

Alice Keck Park Memorial Garden, Micheltorena and Santa Barbara streets—a botanical haven of plants, trees, flowers, streams, and a pond.

Ambassador Park, West Cabrillo Boulevard, opposite West Beach—graced by a double row of palm trees.

Chase Palm Park, East Cabrillo Boulevard—a shoreline park of palm trees named in honor of Pearl Chase, who contributed significantly to the beautiful landscaping and distinctive architecture of the city.

Franceschi Park, Mission Ridge Road—a botanical garden on a former estate.

Mission Rose Garden, Mission Park—fragrant with many kinds of roses set against a backdrop of mission, mountains, and Santa Barbara–style homes.

Shoreline Park, at La Marina and Shoreline Drive, situated along the bluffs above Leadbetter Beach—a park offering fine views of the islands and the harbor.

BOTANIC GARDEN

1212 Mission Canyon Drive, Santa Barbara; (805) 682–4726. Free. Open daily from 8:00 A.M. to sunset; docent tours on Thursday at 10:30 A.M. and Sunday at 11:00 A.M.

Anna Blaksley Bliss established this well-known garden in 1926 in memory of her father. Its focus is California's indigenous flora—flora of the desert, the mountains, and the offshore islands. Five miles of trails display redwood trees, cacti, wildflowers, and other flora. There are also a research library and a gift shop.

CARRIAGE MUSEUM

129 Castillo Street, Santa Barbara; (805) 966–0237. Donation accepted. Open every Sunday from 2:00 to 4:00 P.M.; call to arrange tours at other times.

An intriguing collection of horse-drawn carriages and carts used by Santa Barbara pioneers is on display at this museum; included are buggies, stagecoaches, a firefighting pumper, and even a hearse. During Fiesta Week in August, the carriages are driven through the streets of the city.

EL PRESIDIO DE SANTA BARBARA STATE PARK

123 East Canon Perdido Street, Santa Barbara; (805) 966–9719. Free. Open Monday through Friday from 10:30 A.M. to 4:30 P.M. and Saturday and Sunday from noon to 4:00 P.M.

With the establishment in 1782 of El Presidio (*presidio* refers to a fortified military outpost and habitation), Santa Barbara was founded. El Presidio was one of four original royal forts that were the Spanish empire's outposts in the New World. Today, remains of Santa Barbara's presidio, such as the walls and foundation, are being reconstructed. The chapel has also been lovingly restored and embellished with eighteenth-century decorations. Within the presidio are the padre's (priest's) quarters; El Cuartel (1782), Santa Barbara's oldest building and the second oldest in California; and Caneda Adobe (1782). An audiovisual presentation shows what life was like in early colonial California.

FERNALD HOUSE AND TRUSSEL-WINCHESTER ADOBE

414 West Montecito Street, Santa Barbara; (805) 966–6639. Admission charge. Open Sunday, 2:00 to 4:00 P.M.

This imposing, Victorian-style mansion was built in 1862. It has fourteen beautifully furnished rooms, an elegant staircase, and carved decorations. The Trussel-Winchester Adobe (1854), next door, is built with adobe bricks (*adobe* means heavy clay mixed with straw), wood timber, and brass trimmings that were salvaged from a vessel wrecked off Anacapa Island.

SANTA BARBARA

SANTA BARBARA COUNTY COURTHOUSE
*1100 block of Anacapa Street, Santa Barbara; (805) 681–4200.
Free. Open Monday through Friday from 8:00 A.M. to 5:00 P.M. and
Saturday and Sunday from 9:00 A.M. to 5:00 P.M.*

Santa Barbara's county courthouse, considered one of the most
beautiful public buildings in America, combines both Spanish colonial and Moorish architectural influences. The richly decorated
interior contains huge murals, carved doors, tiles imported from
Spain, wrought-iron chandeliers, and lavishly designed ceilings.
You are welcome to go up into the 70-foot-high clock tower for views
of this red-tile-roofed city, the Pacific, and the mountains. The courthouse is situated on beautifully landscaped grounds.

SANTA BARBARA HISTORICAL MUSEUM
*136 East De La Guerra Street, Santa Barbara; (805) 966–1601. Free.
Open Tuesday through Friday from noon to 5:00 P.M. and Saturday
and Sunday from 1:00 to 5:00 P.M.*

The city's historical museum portrays four eras of settlement—
Chumash Indian, Spanish colonial, Mexican, and American. Two
adobe structures are on museum grounds. The first, Casa de Co-
varrubias (1817), was the site of the last Mexican Assembly meeting,
held in July 1846, and served too as headquarters for Señor Pio Pico,
the last Mexican governor of California. Historic Adobe (1836), the
second house, served as headquarters for Colonel John C. Frémont
after Santa Barbara was taken by U.S. troops in 1846.

SANTA BARBARA MUSEUM OF ART
*1130 State Street, Santa Barbara; (805) 963–4364. Donation ac-
cepted. Open Tuesday through Saturday from 11:00 A.M. to 5:00 P.M.
and Sunday from noon to 5:00 P.M.*

The Santa Barbara Museum of Art, one of the finest smaller
museums in the country, contains an impressive collection of American art, ancient statuary, oriental art, and paintings by European
and American artists.

SANTA BARBARA MUSEUM OF NATURAL HISTORY
*2559 Puesta del Sol Road, Santa Barbara; (805) 682–4711. Free.
Open daily from 9:00 A.M. to 5:00 P.M. (Sunday from 10:00 A.M. to 5:00
P.M.).*

The Museum of Natural History is one of the city's most popular
attractions, especially with children. Its emphasis is on the natural
and human history of the North American West Coast. The museum

127

features a hall of American Indian culture, including a diorama on prehistoric Indian life in the Santa Barbara area, and the skeleton of a giant blue whale.

SANTA BARBARA PUBLIC LIBRARY
40 East Anapamu Street, Santa Barbara; (805) 962–7653. Free. Open Monday through Thursday, 10:00 A.M. to 9:00 P.M.; Friday and Saturday, 10:00 A.M. to 5:30 P.M.; and Sunday, 1:00 to 4:00 P.M.

This attractive, 2-story building houses the Faulkner Gallery, which displays works by area artists and craftspeople, and a collection of scale models of Spanish sailing ships. The library is also a refuge of peace for quiet reading after a day of touring.

SEA CENTER
At Stearns Wharf, Santa Barbara; (805) 963–1067. Admission charge. Summer to Labor Day, open daily from 11:00 A.M. to 7:00 P.M.; the rest of the year, open from noon to 5:00 P.M. on weekdays and from 11:00 A.M. to 5:00 P.M. on Sunday.

The Sea Center, operated by the Santa Barbara Museum of Natural History, has a number of fascinating exhibits on marine life within the Santa Barbara Channel. Among the offerings are a life-size model of a California gray whale, live marine animals in saltwater tanks, and a computer learning center.

SANTA BARBARA ZOO
500 Ninos Drive, Santa Barbara; (805) 962–6310. Free. Open daily from 10:00 A.M. to 5:00 P.M.; summer hours, 10:00 A.M. to 6:00 P.M.

The zoo is located on the grounds of what was previously a private estate, overlooking the ocean and inland bird refuge. It exhibits close to five hundred animals, both native to California and from around the world; here you can find jungle cats, giraffes, elephants, and flamingos. The zoo also has a miniature train ride, a children's petting zoo, a picnic area, and a snack bar.

GOLETA DEPOT RAILROAD MUSEUM
300 Los Carneros Road, Goleta; (805) 964–3540. Donation accepted. Open Monday through Saturday, 1:00 to 4:00 P.M.

This attraction is a favorite with railroad buffs. It displays a 1901 Southern Pacific depot, antique railroad artifacts, old railroading photos and displays, and a 400-square-foot model railroad.

CARPINTERIA VALLEY MUSEUM OF HISTORY

956 Maple Avenue, Carpinteria; (805) 684–3112. Free. Open Tuesday through Friday from 1:30 to 4:00 P.M. and Saturday 11:00 A.M. to 4:00 P.M.

This interesting museum celebrates the heritage of Carpinteria's pioneering families. The artifacts, contributed by descendants of those families, portray how people lived when this area was part of America's frontier. Also on exhibit are such items as an oil boom, farming equipment, a turn-of-the-century schoolroom, and Chumash Indian artifacts.

Santa Barbara County Wineries

A forty-five-minute drive to the north of Santa Barbara, via Highway 101 and/or 154, lies a magnificent countryside of vineyards and wineries, as well as a number of engaging attractions, such as the Santa Ynez Valley Historical Museum, the Chumash Painted Cave Rock (ancient Indian pictographs), the Old Ballard School (1883) in Ballard, the town of Los Olivos with its many antique shops and art galleries, and the community of Solvang. Solvang is a bit of Denmark in Southern California, its Old World charm including Mission Santa Ines (1804), the Hans Christian Andersen Park, and gift shops and restaurants done in Danish motif. Further north, in Lompoc, is a special treat: vast fields carpeted with commercially grown flowers, blooming from early June to mid-July, including sweet peas, asters, calendula, larkspur, lavender, marigolds, and lobelia. Nearby is La Purisma, a superb example of California mission architecture. Also in Santa Barbara's vineyard country is Lake Cachuma County Park, off Highway 154 between Santa Barbara and Solvang (805–688–4658). The lake is stocked with bass, catfish, trout, bluegill, and crappie. At the lake is a bait and tackle shop where you can purchase a fishing license and rent a boat and motor. The park has campsites, picnic areas, a snack bar, and a swimming pool (no swimming in the lake). Wildlife enthusiasts enjoy seasonal cruises on the lake to view migrating bald eagles. A small admission is charged per vehicle for a day's visit.

Most of the wineries listed below welcome visitors between 10:00 A.M. and 4:00 P.M., and all offer tastings of their wine products. For a free touring map and informational brochure, call Santa Barbara County Vintners' Association at (805) 688–0881.

Austin Cellars, Grand Avenue off Highway 154, Los Olivos; (805) 688–9665

Bryon Vineyard and Winery, Tepusquet Road northeast of Highway 101, Santa Maria; (805) 937–7288

Firestone Vineyard, Zaca Station Road off Highway 101, Los Olivos; (805) 688–3940

J. Carey Cellars, Alamo Pintado Road off Highway 154, Solvang; (805) 688–8554

Rancho Sisquoc, Foxen Canyon Road off Highway 101, Santa Maria; (805) 937–3616

Sanford Winery, Santa Rosa Road off Highway 246, Buellton; (805) 688–3300

Santa Barbara Winery, Anacapa Street, Santa Barbara; (805) 963–3633

Vega Vineyards Winery, Santa Rosa Road and Highway 101, Buellton; (805) 688–2415

Zaca Mesa Winery, Foxen Canyon Road off Highway 101, Los Olivos; (805) 688–3310

Santa Barbara Area Accommodations

BEST WESTERN PEPPER TREE INN
3850 State Street, Santa Barbara; (805) 687–5511. Moderate.
　　Very nice rooms with patios overlooking a swimming pool. Amenities include fresh fruit, refrigerators, hair dryers, two swimming pools and a spa, and a health and fitness facility. Located near Santa Barbara's largest shopping center.

BLUE QUAIL INN BED AND BREAKFAST
1908 Bath Street, Santa Barbara; (805) 687–2300. Moderate to expensive.
　　Cottages and suites located near downtown and beaches. Offers fireplaces, patios, bikes, and breakfasts in the rate.

EL ENCANTO HOTEL AND GARDEN VILLAS
1900 Lasuen Road, Santa Barbara; (805) 687–5000 (in California, 800–346–7039). Expensive.
　　Located high in the Santa Barbara foothills, El Encanto features splendid accommodations in cottages that have sweeping views

of the city, the ocean, and Channel Islands. The gardens here are gorgeous, and guest services are first-rate.

FESS PARKER'S RED LION RESORT
633 East Cabrillo Boulevard, Santa Barbara; (805) 564–4333. Expensive.

Fess Parker is the tall, lanky actor who played Walt Disney's version of Davy Crockett in the movies and on television. This first-class resort, located within a few steps of an ocean beach, features large, well-decorated rooms with balconies or patios, a health and fitness facility, a swimming pool and spa, a tennis court, two restaurants and lounges, and other amenities.

FOUR SEASONS BILTMORE AT SANTA BARBARA
1260 Channel Drive, Montecito; (805) 969–2261. Expensive.

Superb accommodations, dining, amenities, and services in a lavish, Spanish colonial environment. Offers two swimming pools, whirlpools, a putting green, tennis courts, a gourmet restaurant, a lounge with entertainment, and afternoon tea.

FRANCISCAN INN
109 Bath Street, Santa Barbara; (805) 963–8845. Moderate.

Comfortable accommodations located one block from the beach. Offers a swimming pool and spa, as well as complimentary continental breakfast.

HARBOUR CARRIAGE HOUSE
420 West Montecito Street, Santa Barbara; (805) 962–8447. Moderate to expensive.

Located two blocks from the beach. Offers rooms with spas and fireplaces, plus full American breakfasts.

MASON BEACH INN
324 West Mason Street, Santa Barbara; (805) 962–3203 or (800) 446–0444. Moderate to expensive.

Located one block from the beach and harbor. Offers deluxe rooms, a swimming pool, a Jacuzzi, and complimentary continental breakfast.

MIRAMAR HOTEL
1555 South Jameson Lane, Montecito; (805) 969–2203. Moderate to expensive.

The only resort directly on the beach. Comfortable accommodations with balconies overlooking the beach and ocean, a restaurant, a lounge, two swimming pools, a spa, tennis courts, and a
health and fitness facility.

MONTECITO INN

*1295 Coast Village Road, Santa Barbara; (805) 969–7854 or (800)
331–3815 (in California, 800–843–2017). Expensive.*

This small hotel was built by Charlie Chaplin as an elegant
retreat for movie stars. Located near the beach and the exclusive
Montecito residential area, the hotel offers fine rooms, a restaurant,
a swimming pool, a health and fitness facility, bikes, free trolley
service to downtown, and many other amenities.

SAN YSIDRO RANCH

900 San Ysidro Lane, Montecito; (805) 969–5046. Expensive.

Many distinguished people—including John F. and Jacqueline
Kennedy, who spent their honeymoon here, and kings and prime
ministers—have been guests at San Ysidro Ranch, one of America's
finest resorts. The ranch's 550 acres are set within the foothills of the
Santa Ynez mountains. Accommodations are in nicely furnished
private cottages; the Stone House dining room serves excellent
meals, or you can have dining service at your cottage. Recreations
include horseback riding, tennis, swimming, dancing, and hiking.
This is the perfect place for those who need privacy in a splendid
environment.

SANTA BARBARA INN

*435 South Milpas Street at Cabrillo Boulevard, Santa Barbara; (805)
966–2285. Moderate to expensive.*

Located near the beach. Offers fine rooms with balconies or
patios, a Don the Beachcomber restaurant and lounge, and dancing and entertainment.

SHERATON SANTA BARBARA HOTEL AND SPA

*111 East Cabrillo Boulevard, Santa Barbara; (805) 963–0744.
Expensive.*

Choice rooms with ocean or mountain views. The hotel is located across the road from the beach. Amenities include a swimming pool, full-service health and fitness facilities, Zack's restaurant,
and a lounge with entertainment.

Santa Barbara Dining

Fresh seafood is at its best in Santa Barbara, and many area restaurants prepare the catch of the day in enticing ways. Some of the top restaurants are at the major hotels. The following dining places are recommended for daily sustenance and enjoyment:

ALEX'S CANTINA
5918 Hollister Street, Santa Barbara; (805) 683–2577. Inexpensive.
Alex's was voted Santa Barbara's best Mexican restaurant, in a poll conducted by the *Santa Barbara Independent.*

BALTIERI'S
5892 Hollister Avenue, Goleta; (805) 967–2881. Inexpensive to moderate.
Soul-satisfying Italian fare, ravioli with marinara sauce or with meatballs or sausages, linguini with clam sauce, veal piccata, and halibut Provençal.

CATTLEMAN'S RESTAURANT
3744 State Street, Santa Barbara; (805) 687–2828. Inexpensive.
Steaks, roast beef, and fresh seafood dishes.

CHALK BOARD
621 State Street, Santa Barbara; (805) 962–2773. Moderate to expensive.
Gourmet cuisine served in a European atmosphere. Specialties include halibut and clam with tarragon and garlic, grilled swordfish with mango and green chili butter, and lamb loin with thyme, balsamie, and tomato.

CHINA CASTLE
1202 Chapala Street, Santa Barbara; (805) 962–6602. Inexpensive.
Authentic Mandarin, Szechwan, and Hunan cuisines. Specialties include vegetarian bear-foot-shaped bean curd, tea-smoked duck, and shrimp in a flower basket.

CITY BROILER
1129 State Street, Santa Barbara; (805) 965–8500. Moderate.
Steaks and seafood, huge portions of prime beef, and several kinds of salads. Jazz entertainment.

COLD SPRING TAVERN
5995 Stage Coach Road, Santa Barbara; (805) 967–0066. Moderate to expensive.
A historic stagecoach tavern. Warm hospitality, good food and wines, and a relaxing atmosphere. Venison, quail, rabbit, and other wild game are among the specialties.

EPICUREAN
125 East Carillo Street, Santa Barbara; (805) 966–4789. Expensive.
One of Santa Barbara's finest gourmet restaurants. Excellent food, service, wines, dining decor, and ambience.

GRILL IN MONTECITO
1279 Coast Village Road, Montecito; (805) 969–5959. Moderate.
An intimate restaurant with candlelit tables. Serves Italian and seafood dishes and offers jazz entertainment.

LOUIE'S
1404 De La Vina Street, Santa Barbara; (805) 963–7003. Moderate.
Excellent California cuisine in the historic Victorian Upham Hotel. Lunches on the porch include gourmet pizzas, fresh fish, and salads.

MICHAEL'S WATERSIDE INN
50 Los Patos Way, Montecito; (805) 969–0307. Expensive.
A superior restaurant housed in a 1872 Victorian cottage. Serves classic and modern French cuisine—petite-cultured abalone, roast duckling with locally grown olives, and raspberry crepe soufflé.

MIMOSA RESTAURANT
2700 De La Vina Street, Santa Barbara; (805) 682–2465. Moderate.
Delicious meals—for example, scallops sautéed with garlic, roast lamb loin, pork scaloppine, New York steak tarragon, veal sweetbreads, and bouillabaisse.

MOBY DICK RESTAURANT
220 Stearns Wharf, Santa Barbara; (805) 965–0549. Moderate.
A variety of fresh seafood dishes. Your table is within a glass porch dining room overlooking the ocean. A favorite place with the local people.

MOUSSE ODILE

18 East Cota Street, Santa Barbara; (805) 962–5393. Moderate to expensive.

Fine French cooking—leg of lamb roasted with garlic and herbs, boned chicken breast with fresh mushrooms and a light champagne sauce, and filet mignon with pepper sauce and cognac.

PAPAGALLO'S

731 De La Guerra Plaza, Santa Barbara; (805) 963–8374. Moderate.

Peruvian specialties served in a fountain courtyard. Well-prepared dishes include paella, soft-shell crabs, and fettuccine Papagallo. South American musical entertainment.

SOMETHING FISHY

720 Chapala Street, Santa Barbara; (805) 963–7760. Moderate to expensive.

A strange name for a superb Japanese restaurant. Tableside Teppan cooking, a bountiful sushi bar, and tempura and Japanese steaks.

YOUR PLACE RESTAURANT

22 North Milpas Street, Santa Barbara; (805) 966–5151. Inexpensive to moderate.

Delicious Siamese soups, curries, seafood—more than a hundred exotic, delicious dishes.

Santa Barbara Area Entertainment

On any given day or evening in the Santa Barbara area, a panoply of entertainment takes place—special events, festivals, theater, and music of all kinds, from classical to popular. Both the Arlington and Lobero theaters are main venues for the city's performing arts organizations and center stage for leading guest artists from around the world. Many of Santa Barbara's hotels and resorts feature live entertainers (singers and comics) in their lounges, as well as offering dinner dancing. In addition, there are many movie houses in town. Ask your hotel concierge or guest relations person for information on current entertainment choices.

Tickets for entertainment events can be purchased through Mistix Ticket Agency (805–682–7024) and Ticket Master (805–965–

3377). Following is a list of performing arts organizations that enrich Santa Barbara.

Access Theatre, (805) 682–8184. Presents plays by disabled and nondisabled actors; all shows in sign language and voiced English.
Ensemble Theatre, (805) 963–0761. Santa Barbara's only resident professional theater company offering classical and modern plays year-round.
Gilbert and Sullivan Company, (805) 969–7400. Delightful G&S shows presented throughout the year.
Music Academy of the West, (805) 969–4726. Summer festival concerts featuring America's best music students and guest artists.
P.C.P.A. Theaterfest, (800) 221–9469. Presents plays in Solvang during the summer and in Santa Maria from January through May.
Repertory-West Dance Company, (805) 961–3241. The University of California at Santa Barbara's resident professional dance company, presenting performances throughout the year.
Santa Barbara Chamber Orchestra, (805) 569–3277. Presents six concerts from October through April.
Santa Barbara Choral Society, (805) 965–7905. A 120-voice group performing works from the baroque to the modern.
Santa Barbara Civic Light Opera, (805) 964–1442. A year-round schedule of musicals and light operas.
Santa Barbara County Bowl, (805) 963–2993. A summertime, outdoor stage for concerts.
Santa Barbara Oratorio Chorale, (805) 964–5823. Three choral concerts with orchestra and soloists presenting works in the oratorio tradition.
Santa Barbara Symphony, (805) 965–6596. A full season of concerts from October to May.

Santa Barbara Shopping

A pleasure in visiting Santa Barbara is strolling the streets downtown and poking around the many interesting shops and art galleries. A popular downtown shopping complex is Victoria Court, which has thirty shops, restaurants, and services tucked along winding paths and inner courtyards. Another is La Cumbre Plaza, with more than sixty stores and restaurants. The Galleria, on the corner of State and La Cumbre Road, is a 2-story complex containing designer boutiques, chic specialty shops, and gourmet food stores. La Arcada

SANTA BARBARA

Court is a Spanish paseo and courtyard decorated with trees, plants, fountains, and walks. Around it is a variety of shops and galleries, and a tall, Westminster chime clock stands at its entrance. El Paseo is a lovely and historic shopping arcade in which there are irresistible shops, art galleries, and restaurants. Piccadilly Square, an enclosed mall with more than thirty-five shops, is nearby. At Brinker-hoff Avenue, named after the city's first doctor, antique and specialty shops are within Victorian-era houses. And in nearby Montecito, Coast Village Road and Montecito Village, located at the intersection of San Ysidro and East Valley Roads, contain a winning collection of shops and restaurants.

9

San Diego:
Beautiful City on the Pacific

San Diego possesses great beauty, one of the best year-round climates in North America, rich culture, and a heritage that dates back to the sixteenth century. This city and its metropolitan area are a favorite vacation destination with travelers worldwide.

San Diego is California's oldest city. The area was discovered in 1542 by Juan Rodriguez Cabrillo, a Portuguese explorer. Missions were established in the eighteenth century by Roman Catholic priests from Spain and Mexico. San Diego, initially a colonial outpost on the Pacific of the Spanish empire, became a growing settlement under Mexican regimes and in the mid-nineteenth century was ceded to the United States following the Mexican War.

The city is part of San Diego County, which also has within it the communities of Carlsbad, Chula Vista, Coronado, Del Mar, El Cajon, Imperial Beach, La Jolla, La Mesa, Lemon Grove, National City, Oceanside, Pacific Beach, Poway, San Marcos, Santee, and Vista. More than 2.2 million persons live in the county, with more than 1.0 million residing in the city of San Diego. San Diego's major industries are military installations (it is the headquarters of the Eleventh Naval District and contains the "Top Gun" Naval fighter aviators' school, as well as a Marine Corps boot camp, for example), manufacturing, government, tourism, education, medicine, finance, retailing, and agriculture. Tourism is one of San Diego's most important industries, providing close to a hundred thousand jobs.

How To Get There

San Diego is located in the southwest corner of California, 120 miles south of Los Angeles and only 20 miles north of Tijuana, Mexico.

BY CAR

San Diego is about a two-and-a-half-hours' trip from downtown Los Angeles via the San Diego Freeway (Interstate 5). Interstate 8 provides access to the city from Arizona and points east. From Palm Springs, San Diego can be reached over the scenic mountain route via Highways 74 to 371 to 79 to Interstate 15 or Highways 86 to 78 to 79 to Interstate 8.

BY AIR

San Diego International Airport, also named Lindbergh Field, is located conveniently next to downtown. It is served by major U.S. airlines, such as USAir, and by regional lines. Airport terminals have all modern amenities for travelers—restaurants, lounges, private clubs, rental-car agencies, newsstands, and so on.

Many hotels provide shuttle service to and from the airport. Various limousine, taxi, and shuttle services are readily available at the airport to take you into the city or to surrounding communities.

BY TRAIN

Amtrak provides daily service (a) from Los Angeles and points north and (b) via Los Angeles from other regions of the United States and from Canada through Via Rail. Amtrak's station is located at the Santa Fe Depot, at Kettner and Broadway (800–USA–RAIL).

BY BUS

Greyhound has daily service to San Diego, through connecting buses, from all regions of the United States and Canada. For bus service information, call Greyhound at (619) 239–9171.

How To Get Around

Downtown San Diego is a relatively compact area and can be toured on foot, with some help now and then from a taxi. Attractions such as Horton Plaza, a 7-block downtown shopping area; the 8-block-long Gaslamp Quarter; the Maritime Museum; Seaport Village; and Embarcadero Marine Park are within this central area. You will need transportation to reach the attractions within Balboa Park, Sea World at Mission Bay, Coronado Beach, La Jolla, Point Loma, and so on.

The main streets of downtown are Broadway (east-west), Harbor Drive (north-south), First Street to Seventh Avenue (north-south), and A to G streets (east-west). Coronado is reached via Highway 75 (Bay Bridge; toll paid only for coming on) off of Harbor Drive or Interstate 5. The Mission Bay area (Sea World), Pacific Beach, and La Jolla are reached via Interstate 5 going north from downtown San Diego. Interstate 5 also leads south to Tijuana, Mexico.

Public transportation is provided by San Diego Transit (619–233–2004); San Diego Trolley (619–231–8549), offering a low-fare shuttle between downtown and Tijuana, Mexico; Diamond or Yellow Cab (619–234–6161); and Orange Cabs (619–219–3337). The Transit Store, at 449 Broadway and Fifth Avenue, provides transportation tickets, passes, and route and touring information.

The following companies offer tours of Greater San Diego:

Baja Frontier Tours, (619) 232–1600
Coronado Trolley Tours, (619) 437–1861
Gray Line Tours, (619) 231–9922
Molly Trolley Express, (619) 233–9177
San Diego Tours, (619) 239–3015
Skysurfer Balloon Company, (619) 481–6800
Flight Trails Helicopters, (619) 438–8424
Pacific Horizon Balloon Tours, (619) 756–1790
Champagne Cowboy Tours, (619) 283–0220
Old Town Walking Tours, (619) 296–1004
Gaslamp Quarter Foundation Walking Tours, (619) 233–5227

Tourism Information

SAN DIEGO INTERNATIONAL INFORMATION CENTER
11 Horton Plaza, First Avenue and F Street
San Diego 92101
(619) 236–1212
Open daily, 8:30 A.M. to 5:30 P.M.; closed Thanksgiving and Christmas. A multilingual staff is available for the convenience of non-English-speaking visitors.

Important Telephone Numbers

Emergencies (Police, Fire, Medical), Dial 911
Doctor Referral, (619) 565–8161
Dentist Referral, (619) 223–5391
Weather, (619) 289–1212
Entertainment Hotline, (619) 234–2787
Time, (619) 853–1212
International Weather and Time Information, (602) 230–2323
Senior Citizens' Information, (619) 236–5765
Travelers' Aid Society, (619) 232–7991

Special Events

JANUARY
Annual Maple Leaf Months (honoring Canadian visitors), January
  through February
MONY Tournament of Champions (PGA golf tournament), mid-
  January
Military Heritage Jamboree, late January

FEBRUARY
Annual Old Mission Beach Rugby Tournament, mid-February
Oceanside Whale Festival, mid-February
Annual San Diego Half Marathon, mid-February
Andy Williams Open (PGA golf tournament), mid-February
Michelob Invitational Indoor Track Meet, late February

MARCH
Ocean Beach Kite Festival, mid-March

APRIL
San Diego Crew Classic (college rowing competition), early April
Peg Leg Liars Contest (storytelling festival), early April
Kyocera Inamori Golf Classic (women's PGA tournament), early
  April
Pacific Beach Spring Art Festival, mid-April
Bud Light La Jolla Grand Prix (bicycle race), mid-April
Annual Downtown Art Walk, late April
Jumping Frog Jamboree (sports for frogs), late April

SAN DIEGO

MAY
Fiesta de la Primavera (the city's Spanish and Mexican festival), in May

Del Mar National Horse Show, early to mid-May

Cinco de Mayo Festival (Mexican celebration), early May

Air/Space America (aerospace trade show), mid-May

Annual Temecula Hot Air Balloon and Wine Tasting Festival, late May

Annual Greek Festival, late May

Annual Billy Bones Schooner Festival, late May

JUNE
Old Globe Theatre Season, June through September

San Diego Symphony Summer Pops Concerts, June through September

Starlight Musicals in Balboa Park, June through October

American Indian Fair, early June

JULY
Annual Sand Castle Days, late July

Del Mar Thoroughbred Club Racing Season, late July to mid-September

AUGUST
Naval Air Station Miramar Air Show (home of the "Top Gun" fliers), in August

Carmel Mountain Ranch Hot Air Balloon Festival, in August

Festival of Chocolate, mid-August

SEPTEMBER
Annual International Seafood Fair, in September

Annual Underwater Film Festival, early September

Annual Miller Highlife Thunderboat Regatta (hydroplane races), mid-September

Annual Fiddle and Banjo Contest, mid-September

Annual San Diego Scottish Highland Games, late September

Cabrillo Festival, late September

OCTOBER
Oktoberfest, late September to early October

Annual Fall Apple Festival, weekends in October

San Diego Power and Sailboat Show, in October

Harvest Festival and Christmas Crafts Market, in mid-October
Southern California Grand Prix (championship car races), mid to
    late October
Ye Olde English Faire, mid-October

NOVEMBER
Baja, Mexico 1,000 KM (the wild and woolly off-road race down the
    Baja peninsula), early November
San Diego Marathon, early November
Annual Great American Dixieland Jazz Festival, late November

DECEMBER
Annual Holiday in the City Parade, in December
Holiday Bowl (college football bowl game), in December
Annual Candlelight Victorian Home Tour, in December
Whale Watching Season, mid-December through February
San Diego Harbor Parade of Lights (parade of yachts and other
    boats), mid-December
Los Posadas (Mexican Christmas celebration at Mission San Luis
    Rey), mid-December

Professional and Recreational Sports

Both the **San Diego Padres** (baseball; 619–283–4494) and the **San Diego Chargers** (football; 619–280–2121) play their games at San Diego Jack Murphy Stadium, 9449 Friars Road in Mission Valley (619–283–5808). The **San Diego Sockers** (soccer; 619–224–4625) have their matches at the San Diego Sports Arena, 3500 Sports Arena Boulevard in San Diego (619–224–4175).

Thoroughbred horse racing is held from late July through mid-September at the Del Mar Race Track, Via de La Valle in Del Mar (619–755–1141). Greyhound and thoroughbred racing takes place throughout the year at the Caliente Race Track, Boulevard Agua Caliente in Tijuana, Mexico (706–681–7811). Jai alai matches are held nightly, except Thursday, at the Fronton Palacio, Avienda Revolucion, Tijuana, Mexico (706–260–0452). Tijuana has two bull-fight rings, and the season runs from early May to early October; call (800) 522–1516 for more information.

Swimming, sunbathing, and other beach sports are best at Pacific Beach, Mission Beach, La Jolla Shores, Mission Bay Park, and Coronado Beach. Mission Bay, Tourmaline Surf Park, and Cardiff-

Balboa Park, the cultural heart of San Diego

by-the-Sea are terrific for sailboarding. Surfboarders favor Windansea in La Jolla, as well as Tourmaline Surf Park. Snorkeling and scuba-diving enthusiasts discover a lot of underwater interest at La Jolla Cove and Underwater Marine Reserve.

There are specially marked bike trails in downtown San Diego and in most of the scenic, coastal towns flanking the city. Bike rentals are available at Pennyfarthings, 520 Fifth Avenue in San Diego (619–233–7696); Hamel's in Mission Beach (619–488–5050); Alpine in Pacific Beach (619–273–0440); and La Jolla Cyclery in La Jolla (619–233–7696).

San Diego is oriented to the sea. If you have the time, go out on the bay or ocean. Boat rentals can be arranged at California Pacific Sailing Sports (619–270–3211), Coronado Boat Rental (619–437–1514), Seaforth Boat Rentals (619–223–1681), and Mission Bay Sports Center (619–488–1004).

A deep-sea fishing trip out on the Pacific can top off a great trip for many folks. These companies provide everything—boat, gear, bait, beer, food: Seaforth Sportsfishing (619–224–3383), H and M Sportfishing (619–222–1144), and Point Loma Sportfishing (619–223–1627).

The Greater San Diego area has more than seventy golf courses, many of them open to visitors. The Torrey Pines Municipal Golf Course, site of the PGA Andy Williams San Diego Open in February, is one of the best. Torrey has two eighteen-hole, par 72 courses; is located at 11480 North Torrey Pines Road in La Jolla (619–453–0380). The San Diego Convention and Visitors Bureau (619–232–3101) will suggest other courses.

The best place for jogging/running in downtown San Diego is Balboa Park. And in the San Diego area are hundreds of public and private tennis courts, twenty-five of them in Balboa Park (619–298–0920). Many hotels, such as the Hotel del Coronado, have their own courts. For more information on playing tennis, call the Visitors Bureau at the above number or ask your hotel concierge.

Sea World of California

Location: 1720 South Shores Road in the Mission Bay area of San Diego. Driving from the north or south, take Exit West from Interstate 5 onto Sea World Drive; driving from the east—Interstate 8—take West Mission Bay Drive to Sea World Drive East.
Telephone Information: (619) 226–3901

SAN DIEGO

Mailing Address: 1720 South Shores Road, Mission Bay, San Diego, 92109

Cost: Admission includes all shows and exhibits. Lower rates are available for seniors and children ages three through eleven. Special-rate twelve-month passes are also available.

Hours of Operation: Open daily from 9:00 A.M. to dusk. Hours are extended during summer and holiday periods.

Peak Visiting Periods: Summer months, school vacations, long holiday periods, and weekends.

Time to See Everything: One full day.

Guest Amenities: Free parking, stroller and wheelchair rentals, guided tours, educational programs, plus many restaurants and shops. The attraction also offers camera rentals, film processing, handicapped services, lockers, lost and found, and picnic facilities.

WHAT TO SEE AND DO

Sea World of California, which celebrated its twenty-fifth anniversary in 1988, is America's premier marine life entertainment park. Opened on twenty-two acres in 1964 by four UCLA fraternity brothers, Sea World of California is today spread out on 135 acres. Since its beginning, this popular Southern California attraction has had more than 50 million paying guests. Other Sea Worlds are located in Orlando, Florida, and San Antonio, Texas.

Sea World of California features seven shows, four aquariums, thirty educational exhibits, and several rides.

The most popular show is Shamu and his killer whale companions, which do astounding tricks in a tank holding 6 million gallons of saltwater. Other shows include New Friends, enlivened by dolphins and a pilot whale; the Sea Lion and Otter Show; City Streets, a musical variety show featuring world-class skateboarders and bike riders; Muscle Beach, a high-dive act with comedy; Sparkletts Water Fantasy, a computerized light, music, and water extravaganza; Japanese Village Pearl Diving, in which Japanese girls (amas) dive for pearl-bearing oysters in a 16-foot-deep pool; and Sea World Summer Nights, consisting of such special events as fireworks, musical groups, novelty entertainment acts, and dinner buffets. During summer evenings, there is also an ice-skating show at Nautilus Amphitheater.

Sea World's aquariums contain live sharks, fish, and marine invertebrates from around the world and freshwater fish from the Amazon, Africa, and Asia. Four 55,000-gallon pools feature large kelp-bed fish, a tropical coral reef, schooling fish, and game fish.

Among the thirty educational marine exhibits are a whale and dolphin petting pool, a pool of rare Commerson dolphins, a California tidal pool, walrus exhibits, and exotic birds from around the world. Penguin Encounter is a unique exhibit in which seven different species of penguins inhabit a state-of-the-art facility.

In addition to the shows, aquariums, and exhibits are these other attractions: Places of Learning, highlighting new educational materials of interest to parents and children; beautiful gardens throughout the park, displaying some 3,500 species of plants from throughout the world; Skytower, providing fantastic views of San Diego; and Skyride, offering a gondola ride across Mission Bay (separate charge for rides).

Sea World has a special entertainment area just for children. Called Cap'n Kids' World, it features King of the Wave, the Bounding Main, Swashbuckler's Swing, and more.

Balboa Park

BALBOA PARK
Via Highway 163 North from downtown, Cabrillo Freeway.
Balboa Park is San Diego's huge (1,074 acres) green space of beautiful gardens, museums, theaters, picnic and recreational areas, the world-famous San Diego Zoo, and tranquil walking or jogging paths. Balboa Park was the site of two international expositions, in 1915 and 1936. The Prado is the park's main thoroughfare, along which are several museums, among them the Museum of Man and the San Diego Museum of Art, both of which are housed in ornate Spanish colonial buildings. **Passport to Balboa Park,** a discount admission ticket to four museums in the park, can be purchased at participating museums or at the Information Center in the House of Hospitality, 1549 El Prado in Balboa Park (619–232–2053).

SAN DIEGO ZOO
2920 Zoo Drive, Balboa Park, San Diego; (619) 234–3153. Admission charge. Open daily from 9:00 A.M.; call for closing times, which change seasonally.
The San Diego Zoo is one of the great zoological parks and animal research facilities in the world. The zoo consists of 100 acres landscaped as a beautiful garden of innumerable botanicals. It has more than 3,200 animals representing 777 species, many of which

are rare and exotic to North America; examples are golden monkeys on loan from China, Komodo dragons from Asia, and koalas from Australia. Also among the zoo's attractions is a three-acre tropical rain forest containing ten animal exhibits set in lush vegetation. Double-deck bus tours, a children's zoo, and a Skyfari aerial tramway are additional offerings.

SAN DIEGO MUSEUM OF ART
(619) 232–7931. Admission charge. Open Tuesday through Sunday, 10:00 A.M. to 4:30 P.M.
A superior collection of Dutch, Flemish, Italian, and Spanish art, Renaissance and baroque, and works by contemporary artists.

TIMKEN ART GALLERY
(619) 239–5548. Free. Open Tuesday through Saturday from 10:00 A.M. to 4:30 P.M. and Sunday from 1:30 to 4:30 P.M.
Orthodox Russian icons, as well as paintings by European and American masters.

MUSEUM OF PHOTOGRAPHIC ARTS
(619) 239–5262. Admission charge. Open daily, 10:00 A.M. to 5:00 P.M. (Thursday until 9:00 P.M.)
Fine art photographs from the masters, new contemporary photography, and special exhibitions.

AEROSPACE MUSEUM
(619) 234–8291. Admission charge. Open daily, 10:00 A.M. to 4:30 P.M.
Exhibits of American and foreign aircraft, as well as space gear.

MUSEUM OF SAN DIEGO HISTORY
(619) 232–6226. Admission charge. Open Wednesday through Sunday, 10:00 A.M. to 4:30 P.M.
Presents the history of this dynamic and beautiful city from the early 1800s to the present.

SAN DIEGO MODEL RAILROAD MUSEUM
(619) 696–0100. Admission charge. Open Friday from 11:00 A.M. to 4:00 P.M. and Saturday and Sunday from 11:00 A.M. to 5:00 P.M.
Housed in El Casa de Balboa, this museum has four large model railroad exhibits.

SAN DIEGO HALL OF CHAMPIONS

(619) 234–2544. Admission charge. Open Monday through Saturday from 10:00 A.M. to 4:30 P.M. and Sunday from noon to 5:00 P.M.
Displays the memorabilia of San Diego's champion athletes. Offers screening of sports films and a new golf exhibit.

SAN DIEGO MUSEUM OF MAN

(619) 239–2001. Admission charge. Open daily, 10:00 A.M. to 4:30 P.M.
Exhibits on the cultures and peoples of Southern California. Special exhibitions in the past have included the Rockefeller collection of Mexican folk art.

NATURAL HISTORY MUSEUM

(619) 232–3821. Free; admission charge for special exhibitions. Open daily, 10:00 A.M. to 4:30 P.M.
Has dinosaur skeletons, Hall of Desert Ecology, and other interesting exhibits.

REUBEN H. FLEET SPACE THEATER AND SCIENCE CENTER

(619) 238–1168. Admission charge. Open daily, 9:45 A.M. to 9:30 P.M.
A wide variety of hands-on, interactive science exhibits and a large-screen Omnimax theater that shows astounding films, making you feel you're a part of the action.

OTHER ATTRACTIONS

Other Balboa Park attractions are Centro Cultural del la Raza, promoting Mexican, American Indian, and Chicano cultures; the House of Pacific Relations, celebrating the cultures of more than twenty-five ethnic groups from around the world; the Old Globe Theatre; the San Diego Art Institute; San Diego Junior Theatre; the Spanish Village Arts and Crafts Center; the Starlight Bowl, offering summer musicals outdoors; the United Nations Building; the Marie Hitchcock Puppet Theater; Spreckles Organ Pavilion; the Alcazar Garden; Zoro Garden; the Botanical Building and Lily Pond; the Cactus Garden; and the Inez Grant Parker Memorial Rose Garden.

There are restaurants in the park—Cafe del Rey Moro, with its fourteenth-century Spanish-Moorish decor, and Sculpture Garden Cafe—and dozens of fast-food stands. Balboa Park also has special attractions just for children: Butterfly rides, a merry-go-round, and a miniature train that travels around a half-mile track.

San Diego Harbor

The entrance to one of the world's most beautiful harbors, vying with the likes of those in San Francisco, Hong Kong, and Vancouver, lies between Point Loma and Coronado. The city's modern skyline, seen from the water, is impressive. San Diego is a major port for cruise and cargo ships and for military vessels; surrounding the bay are a number of U.S. Navy installations. The best vantage points from which to see the harbor and city skyline are Coronado, Shelter Island, and Point Loma. Shelter Island, often missed by visitors, is located just past the airport on the way to Point Loma, via Highway 209; the island, attached to the mainland by a short causeway, has parks, fishing piers, marinas, places of accommodation, shops, and several restaurants.

Water tours of the harbor are offered by San Diego Harbor Excursions (619–234–4111) and Invader Cruises (619–234–TOUR). Next to the Broadway Pier is the Maritime Museum, which includes among its exhibits the windjammer *Star of India* and the steam ferry *Berkeley*. The San Diego Ferry carries passengers and bikes across the bay to the popular resort area of Coronado. The trip takes about fifteen minutes and departs from Broadway Pier; the ferry runs hourly.

While in San Diego, take a three-hour cruise to watch California gray whales migrate during the winter months. Whale-watching trips are offered by the San Diego Natural History Museum (619–232–3821), Invader Cruises (619–234–8687), San Diego Harbor Excursion (619–234–4111), and Fisherman's Landing (619–222–0391).

Other Attractions

MISSION BAY

Located north of downtown, Mission Bay is a recreational playground offering boating, fishing, board sailing, and ocean swimming. In this area there are miles of beaches, miles of paths for biking and running, and areas for picnicking, flying kites, or simply lounging in the sun. Sea World is also located at Mission Bay.

SAN DIEGO WILD ANIMAL PARK

15500 San Pasqual Valley Road, Escondido; (619) 234–6541. Admission charge. Call for schedule, as hours change with the season.

SAN DIEGO

San Diego Wild Animal Park is a 1,800-acre preserve, located 30 miles north of San Diego, that allows animals from Africa, Asia, and other continents to roam freely as they would in their native habitats. Visitors get a close look at these exotic animals by riding the Wagasa Bush Line Monorail, with a guide providing narration. The Kilimanjaro Hiking Trail takes you past lions, tigers, elephants, and other intriguing animals. The park has a bonsai exhibit, said to be the largest in the western United States, and its Baja Garden features hundreds of rare plants from Mexico. At Nairobi Village you can see magnificent lowland gorillas; at the Animal Care Center you can watch tender loving care being given to young animals.

CABRILLO NATIONAL MONUMENT
Located at land's end, Point Loma, reached via Highway 209; (619) 557–5450. Admission charge. Call for a schedule of special programs and bird-watching walks.

This historical monument commemorates the European discovery of the coast of California in 1542 by Juan Rodriguez Cabrillo. The Cabrillo Monument and Old Point Loma Lighthouse offer excellent views of San Diego Harbor, the coastline, and the Pacific Ocean. Also from here you can sometimes see the giant gray whales as they migrate.

OLD TOWN STATE HISTORIC PARK
Old Town, at the northwest end of present-day downtown, is where San Diego began in 1769 with Padre Serra's mission and the Royal Presidio. Six blocks have been designated a historic park, within which are heritage residences, churches, museums, and gardens. Also in this colorful district are souvenir and specialty shops and Mexican restaurants. Bazaar del Mundo, a popular shopping and dining area in Old Town, contains such shops as Artes de Mexico, Libros Bookstore, Guatemala Shop, Brazos Beef Emporium, Design Center Accessories, Ariana, Just Animals, the Gallery, and Geppetto's. Daily tours of Old Town depart at 2:00 P.M. from the Machado y Silvas Adobe, located across the plaza. For more information, call Old Town State Park at (619) 237–6770.

JUNIPERO SERRA MUSEUM
2727 Presidio Drive, Presidio Park; (619) 297–3258. Admission charge. Open Tuesday through Saturday from 10:00 A.M. to 4:30 P.M. and Sunday from noon to 4:30 P.M.

SAN DIEGO

Here one of California's first Roman Catholic missions was established in the mid-eighteenth century by Padre Junípero Serra, a founder of Old California; the first Royal Presidio (fort) was also built here. The museum displays many important historical artifacts from San Diego's Spanish colonial period and is located on a hill offering fine views of beautiful Mission Valley.

In the Greater San Diego area are several Spanish colonial-period missions that are well worth visiting for their historical and architectural significance. The most important of these is Mission Basilica San Diego De Alcala, at 10818 San Diego Mission Road in San Diego (619–281–8449; open daily, 9:00 A.M. to 5:00 P.M.; admission charge), which, founded in 1769, was the first of Padre Serra's necklace of twenty-one missions in Alta California. Two other noteworthy missions are Mission San Antonio De Pala (1816), in Pala, (619–742–3317), and Mission San Luis Rey De Francia (1798), in Oceanside (619–757–3651).

GASLAMP QUARTER
Island Avenue area. Free access. Call (619) 233–5227 for more information.

This 16-block downtown historic district re-creates the spirit and look of San Diego's Victorian past. Many of its nineteenth-century buildings have been restored and now house restaurants, boutiques, antique shops, and offices. Walking tours of the Gaslamp Quarter are offered on Saturdays and depart from the William Heath Davis House, at 410 Island Avenue (619–233–5227).

PALOMAR OBSERVATORY
In Cleveland National Forest. Via Interstate 15 North and Highway 76 East; (619) 742–3476. Free. Open daily, 9:00 A.M. to 4:30 P.M.

Palomar is world famous for its 200-inch reflecting telescope. There is also a small museum here. The best part of coming to Palomar—65 miles to the northeast of San Diego—is the trip up the mountain (about 7,000 feet above sea level), with lots of hairpin turns and panoramic vistas. The observatory is within Cleveland National Forest, a major wilderness recreation area.

SCRIPPS AQUARIUM AND MUSEUM
8602 La Jolla Shores Drive, La Jolla; (619) 534–FISH. Free. Open daily, 9:00 A.M. to 5:00 P.M.

Scripps has a fine aquarium—twenty-two tanks of various fish and marine animals—and also offers lectures and films. The prestigious Scripps Institution of Oceanography is in this area.

Also in La Jolla and near the aquarium are the Salk Institute, which offers docent-led tours of this world-famous medical facility, and the beautiful campus of the University of California at San Diego.

SEAPORT VILLAGE

849 West Harbor Road, San Diego; (619) 235–6568. Free access and free parking. Open from morning until into the night.

Seaport Village, located on fourteen acres along the Embarcadero in downtown, is San Diego's picturesque waterfront dining and shopping complex. The architecture re-creates a nineteenth-century look. Seaport Village has sixty shops, boutiques, and galleries; thirteen theme restaurants; and four major dining places.

LA JOLLA MUSEUM OF CONTEMPORARY ART

700 Prospect Street, La Jolla; (619) 454–0267. Admission charge. Open Tuesday through Sunday from 10:00 A.M. to 5:00 P.M. (Wednesday until 9:00 P.M.).

A "must visit" museum of modern painting, sculpture, photography, industrial design, and graphic art.

HERITAGE PARK

At Juan and Harney streets; call (619) 565–5928 for more information. Free access.

A historic district preserving nineteenth-century San Diego.

MARITIME MUSEUM

1306 North Harbor Drive, San Diego; (619) 234–9153. Admission charge. Open daily, 9:00 A.M. to 8:00 P.M.

Excellent exhibits of maritime artifacts, plus three historic vessels: *Star of India*, a windjammer; the ferryboat *Berkeley*; and the steam yacht *Medea*.

CHULA VISTA NATURE CENTER

1000 Gunpowder Point Drive, Chula Vista; (619) 422–BIRD; Donation accepted. Open Tuesday through Sunday, 10:00 A.M. to 5:00 P.M. Shuttle bus runs to center five minutes after the hour and after the half-hour (fare charged); park at E Street and Bay Boulevard.

LAWRENCE WELK MUSEUM
8860 Lawrence Welk Drive, Escondido; (619) 749–2737. Free. Open daily, 10:30 A.M. to 5:00 P.M.

Memorabilia of the life and career of the master of "champagne music."

CHILDREN'S MUSEUM OF SAN DIEGO
La Jolla Village Square, La Jolla; (619) 450–0767. Admission charge. Open Wednesday through Sunday from noon to 5:00 P.M. and Saturday from 10:00 A.M. to 5:00 P.M.

A super hands-on museum for kids.

FIREHOUSE MUSEUM
1572 Columbia Street, San Diego; (619) 232–FIRE. Free. Open Thursday through Sunday, 10:00 A.M. to 4:00 P.M.

Exhibits of antique firefighting equipment.

MINGEII INTERNATIONAL MUSEUM
4405 La Jolla Village Drive, La Jolla; (619) 453–5300. Admission charge. Open Tuesday through Saturday from 11:00 A.M. to 5:00 P.M. (Friday until 9:00 P.M.).

Outstanding folk art museum.

Baja California

Just 20 miles to the south of San Diego is the city of Tijuana, Mexico, and beyond that the seacoast resort towns of Rosarito Beach and Ensenada. For trips into Mexico it is recommended that you take either a tour bus or the San Diego Trolley (619–231–8549), which departs from the Santa Fe Station downtown every quarter-hour. The trolley takes you to the border, and there you connect with other transportation for the short ride into the city. If you do take your car, you must purchase Mexican liability insurance; this essential-to-have insurance is available from agencies on the American side of the border. You also need a Mexican tourist card and proof of citizenship (American, Canadian, or otherwise), if your trip in Mexico lasts more than three days or you travel more than 75 miles into the country. A U.S. citizen can return with $400 worth of duty-free goods, plus one liter of liquor. Occasionally, crossing back into the United States can entail a lengthy wait because of heavy traffic on weekends or intensive checks for illegal drugs.

Tijuana is a shopper's paradise, with many bargains to be found on brand-name goods (Swiss watches, British woolens and china, etc.) and on the best-obtainable Mexican handicrafts. Most of the top stores are found on Avenida de la Revolucion. There are also scores of excellent restaurants— Mexican, seafood, and continental. The Tijuana Tourism and Convention Bureau will gladly answer your questions and send you information; call them at (800) 522–1516.

Accommodations

Greater San Diego has more than thirty-five thousand rooms in deluxe hotels, budget places, swank resorts, and bed-and-breakfast establishments. The following services can assist you in making arrangements for various kinds of accommodations:

Accommodations and Tour Bureau of San Diego, 1130 Sixth Avenue, San Diego 92101; (619) 226–8100. Hotel packages that include admission to attractions.
Baja Reservations, 3939 La Salle Street, San Diego 92110; (619) 222–9099. Makes hotel, resort, vacation home, and condo arrangements for holidays in Tijuana, Mexico.
Budget Vacations, 4440 Pacific Highway, San Diego 92110; (619) 296–6333 or (800) 225–9610 (in California, 800–824–3051). Specializes in budget accommodations throughout the San Diego area.
Carolyn's Bed and Breakfast Homes, San Diego, 416 Third Avenue, Chula Vista 92010; (619) 422–7009.

BAHIA RESORT HOTEL
998 West Mission Bay Drive, San Diego; (619) 488–0551 or (800) 821–3619 (in California, 800–542–6010). Moderate to expensive.
Quality accommodations on Mission Bay, near Sea World and ocean beaches. Offers a restaurant, a lounge, live entertainment, tennis, a swimming pool, and water-sports equipment rentals and lessons.

BEACH COTTAGES
4225 Ocean Boulevard, San Diego; (619) 483–7670. Moderate.
Accommodation units on Pacific Beach. A family-oriented hotel.

BED AND BREAKFAST INN AT LA JOLLA
910 Draper Avenue, La Jolla; (619) 456–2066. Moderate to expensive.

Nice accommodations near the ocean. Offers fireplaces and ocean views in some rooms, a garden, and continental breakfast.

BEST WESTERN BLUE SEA LODGE
707 Pacific Beach Drive, San Diego; (619) 483–4700 or (800) BLUESEA. Expensive.

Quality oceanfront accommodations; units with kitchens available. Offers a swimming pool, a beach, and complimentary continental breakfast.

BEST WESTERN BEACH TERRACE INN
2775 Ocean Street, Carlsbad; (619) 729–5951 or (800) 433–5415 (in California, 800–662–3224). Moderate to expensive.

On-the-beach rooms and suites. Offers ocean views, kitchens, fireplaces, a swimming pool, and continental breakfast. Near restaurants and shops.

BEST WESTERN BEACH VIEW INN
3180 Carlsbad Boulevard, Carlsbad; (619) 729–1151 or (800) 535–5588 (in California, 800–232–2488). Moderate to expensive.

Located across from the state beach. Offers fine accommodations, a restaurant, a lounge, and a swimming pool.

CARLSBAD INN BEACH AND TENNIS RESORT
3001 Carlsbad Boulevard, Carlsbad; (619) 434–6095 or (800) 235–3939 (in California, 800–874–2431). Moderate to expensive.

Oceanfront accommodations (rooms, suites, and condos). Features a restaurant, a swimming pool, tennis, a health and fitness facility, and a cocktail lounge.

CATAMARAN RESORT HOTEL
3999 Mission Boulevard, San Diego; (619) 488–1081 or (800) 821–3619 (in California, 800–542–6010). Moderate to expensive.

Located on Mission Bay and near Sea World. Amenities include a restaurant, a lounge, dancing, live jazz and sixties music, a swimming pool, a beach, and water sports.

COLONIAL INN HOTEL
910 Prospect Street, La Jolla; (619) 454–2181 or (800) 832–5525. Expensive.

A premium downtown hotel at which rates include full breakfast and a newspaper. Features a swimming pool and Putnam's, the hotel's fine restaurant and bar.

DANA INN AND MARINA
1710 West Mission Bay Drive, San Diego; (619) 222–6440 or (800) 445–3339. Moderate.

On Mission Bay and near Sea World and beaches. Offers a marina, water-sports equipment rentals, tennis, and other recreations.

DOUBLETREE HOTEL OF SAN DIEGO
901 Camino del Rio South, San Diego; (619) 543–9000 or (800) 528–0444. Expensive.

A top-of-the-line luxury hotel, offering excellent accommodations and services, a swimming pool, the Monterey Whaling Company Restaurant, a lounge, and a health and fitness facility. Convenient to attractions, shopping, and beaches.

EMBASSY SUITES HOTEL OF LA JOLLA
4550 La Jolla Village Drive, La Jolla; (619) 453–0400 or (800) EMBASSY. Expensive.

Top-quality suite accommodations. Also included in the rate are complimentary full breakfasts, cocktails, the swimming pool, and other amenities.

EXECUTIVE HOTEL AND ATHLETIC CLUB
1055 First Avenue, San Diego; (619) 232–6141 or (800) 662–4477 (in California, 800–932–4848). Expensive.

Good accommodations in a central location. The outstanding feature of this hotel is its excellent health and fitness facility—handball and racquetball courts, Nautilus equipment, a spa, a steam room, and an aerobics room with instruction. The hotel has a restaurant and other guest amenities.

GLORIETTA BAY INN
1630 Glorietta Boulevard, Coronado; (619) 435–3101 or (800) 854–3380 (in California, 800–432–7045). Moderate to expensive.

Nice accommodations in the historic John Spreckels mansion. Near the Hotel del Coronado, the beach, restaurants, and shopping; free continental breakfast and parking provided.

HORTON GRAND HOTEL
311 Island Avenue, San Diego; (619) 544–1886. Expensive.

A romantic, Victorian-style hotel located in downtown's colorful Gaslamp Quarter. Some rooms feature a brass bed, a fireplace, lace curtains, and antique furnishings. Fine dining in Ida Bailey's Restaurant, and cocktails in the Palace Bar. Near Seaport Village and Horton Plaza.

HOTEL DEL CORONADO
1500 Orange Avenue, Coronado; (619) 522–8000. Expensive.

The Hotel del Coronado, known to sophisticated travelers as the Del, is not just another luxury hotel—it is a famous, glamorous national landmark that in 1988 celebrated its hundredth birthday. Its many towers, turrets, and cupolas make it distinctive among the great hotels of North America; it is certainly unique in Southern California. If you have seen the Marilyn Monroe, Tony Curtis, and Jack Lemmon movie *Some Like It Hot,* you'll be interested to know most of the scenes were filmed at the Hotel del Coronado. Through its long history, the hotel has had the world's rich and famous as guests, including presidents and movie stars (in the case of Ronald Reagan, it has had both in one person).

Although of Victorian vintage, the hotel has been brought up to date in terms of guest comforts and amenities. Among its resort offerings are an oceanfront location with a sand beach, two swimming pools, illuminated championship tennis courts, and physical fitness facilities. The hotel's dining rooms include the formal, beautiful Crown Room, which is well regarded for superb dining and service; the Prince of Wales Restaurant, exuding proper British ambience; and the Ocean Terrace, for drinks and light meals. The hotel also has on its premises several fashionable shops selling such items as cashmere sweaters, resort apparel, furs, jewelry, fancy chocolates, British wares, and children's toys. The landscaping and public areas here are lovely.

HOWARD JOHNSON HOTEL
1430 Seventh Avenue, San Diego; (619) 696–0911 or (800) 654–2000. Moderate.

Good accommodations located near Balboa Park attractions, Seaport Village, and Horton Plaza. Has a restaurant and swimming pool.

HYATT ISLANDIA

1441 Quivira Road, San Diego; (619) 224–1234 or (800) 228–9000. Expensive.

Located in the Mission Bay area and close to Sea World. This Hyatt features excellent accommodations, dining, and services, as well as a swimming pool, sportfishing, sailing, jogging trails, complimentary transportation to Sea World, and lounges with entertainment. Rooms have balconies or decks for water views.

LA COSTA HOTEL AND SPA

Costa del Mar Road, Carlsbad; (619) 438–9111 or (800) 854–6564 (in California, 800–542–6200). Expensive.

La Costa is an internationally known vacation spa. It offers luxury accommodations and gourmet dining, together with golf, tennis, health and recreation facilities, a swimming pool, and many other fine guest amenities. The hotel has top restaurants, plus lounges.

LA JOLLA MARRIOTT

4240 La Jolla Village Drive, La Jolla; (619) 587–1414 or (800) 831–4004. Expensive.

Offers choice accommodations and dining, a health and fitness facility, a swimming pool, a lounge, and numerous other guest amenities.

LE MERIDIEN SAN DIEGO AT CORONADO

2000 Second Street, Coronado; (619) 435–3000 or (800) 543–4300. Expensive.

A new luxury hotel in chic Coronado. Features excellent accommodations and dining, a European-style health club and spa, six tennis courts, minibars and other excellent amenities in guest rooms, and proximity to a golf course.

OMNI SAN DIEGO HOTEL

910 Broadway Circle, San Diego; (619) 239–2200 or (800) THE–OMNI. Expensive.

Luxury accommodations located at downtown's Horton Plaza. Offers tennis courts, a swimming pool, a restaurant, and a lounge.

PELICAN COVE INN BED AND BREAKFAST

320 Walnut Avenue, Carlsbad; (619) 434–5995. Moderate to expensive.

A small inn located a few steps from the beach and near restaurants and shops. Offers feather beds, fireplaces, continental breakfast, afternoon sherry, bikes, beach chairs, and picnic baskets.

SAN DIEGO HILTON BEACH AND TENNIS RESORT

1775 East Mission Bay Drive, San Diego; (619) 276–4010 or (800) HILTONS. Expensive.

A luxury resort located in the Mission Bay area, near Sea World; excellent accommodations and dining. Amenities include tennis, health and fitness facilities, a swimming pool, a lounge, entertainment, cruises on the *Hilton Queen Paddlewheeler*, shops, and lots more.

SAN DIEGO MARRIOTT HOTEL & MARINA

333 West Harbor Drive, San Diego; (619) 234–1500 or (800) 831–4004. Expensive.

The two-tower San Diego Marriott is a superb hotel in an ideal location, adjacent to the Convention Center and Seaport Village on the bay. The rooms are deluxe. Be sure to ask for a bay-view room with a balcony—the sunsets over the water are breathtaking. The hotel offers twenty-four-hour room service, two swimming pools, and a 446-slip marina (come in with your yacht). Restaurants include Molly's, for oversize prime roast beef; Marina Sea Grille, for fresh lobster and shrimp; and Las Cascadas, for huge buffets. DW's Pub is a relaxing bay-view place for cocktails and live jazz entertainment. On the premises is a gift shop, hair salon, and florist.

SAN DIEGO PRINCESS

1404 West Vacation Road, San Diego; (619) 274–4630 or (800) 542–6275. Expensive.

Luxury accommodations on Mission Bay and near Sea World. A romantic tropical atmosphere, offering such amenities as a restaurant, a lounge with entertainment, minibars in rooms, a beach, and tennis, sailing, and biking.

SAN DIEGO RADISSON HOTEL

1433 Camino del Rio South, San Diego; (619) 260–0111 or (800) 247–0075. Moderate to expensive.

161

Luxury accommodations located across from Fashion Valley Mall and five minutes from Sea World. Amenities include a swimming pool and whirlpool, VIP floors offering extra services, a restaurant and lounge, and free transportation to the airport and Fashion Valley Mall.

TORREY PINES INN
11480 North Torrey Pines Road, La Jolla; (619) 453–4420 or (800) 448–8355. Moderate to expensive.
Offers fine accommodations and dining, as well as a golf course. Near the beach.

U. S. GRANT HOTEL
326 Broadway, San Diego; (619) 232–3121 or (800) 237–5029. Expensive.
A top-quality hotel that is listed in the National Register of Historic Places. Located in the center of downtown San Diego, with views of the harbor. Offers fine accommodations, two restaurants, a lounge with entertainment, an exercise room, and many other guest amenities.

WESTGATE
1055 Second Avenue, San Diego; (619) 238–1818. Expensive.
Luxury accommodations in one of San Diego's finest downtown hotels. Amenities include two-line speakerphones with connections for computers, luxury car service to attractions and business meetings, and superb dining at Le Fontainbleau. The decor and guest services are world class.

San Diego Area Campgrounds

You can book campsites at area parks by calling the San Diego County Department of Parks and Recreation at (619) 565–3600 or the California State Parks and Recreation Department at (800) 446–7275.

Border State RV Park, 4141 San Ysidro Boulevard, San Diego; (619) 428–4411—179 sites near beaches and the Mexico border.
Campland on the Bay, 2211 Pacific Beach Drive, San Diego; (619) 581–4200—700 sites on Mission Bay near Sea World.

SAN DIEGO

De Anza Harbor Resort, 2727 De Anza Road, San Diego; (619) 273–3211—250 sites on Mission Bay near Sea World.
San Diego KOA Kampground, 111 North Second Avenue, Chula Vista; (619) 427–3601—270 sites near Sea World and Mexico.

Dining

An excellent source of information on Greater San Diego restaurants is *San Diego Magazine*, a monthly available at newsstands and hotels.

ABBEY RESTAURANT
2825 Fifth Avenue, San Diego; (619) 291-4779. Moderate.
Fine dining in a historical landmark. Offers California cuisine, a broad wine list, and Sunday brunch. Open after theater.

ANTHONY'S FISH GROTTO HARBORSIDE
1355A North Harbor Drive, San Diego; (619) 232–6358. Moderate.
A top San Diego seafood restaurant, featuring the popular "Garden of the Sea" salad bar. Live entertainment in the Sunset Lounge.

AZTEC DINING ROOM
2811 San Diego Avenue, San Diego; (619) 295–2965. Inexpensive.
The restaurant, offering a wide selection of savory Mexican dishes, has been in business since 1937. Live entertainment on weekends.

CALLIOPE'S GREEK CAFE
3958 Fifth Avenue, San Diego; (619) 291–5588. Moderate.
Traditional Greek dishes are terrific at Calliope's—lamb *souvlakia, spanakopeta,* moussaka, as well as fresh seafood.

CHART HOUSE
1701 Strand Way, Coronado; (619) 435–0155. Moderate.
Romantic dining on a patio overlooking Glorietta Bay and the ocean. Offers a wide selection of fresh seafood dishes.

CHINA CAMP
2137 Pacific Highway, San Diego; (619) 232–1367. Moderate.

A top San Diego Chinese restaurant within an early California environment, specializing in Cantonese, Szechwan, and Mandarin cooking.

COPACABANA RESTAURANT OF RIO DE JANEIRO
2888 Pacific Highway, San Diego; (619) 297–COPA. Moderate.
Brazilian food from the rotisserie. The all-inclusive price includes a nightclub show.

DANSK TEA ROOM
8425 La Mesa Boulevard, La Mesa; (619) 463–0640. Moderate.
This is the place to fill your plate again and again from a bountiful Scandinavian smorgasbord.

EL TECOLOTE
6110 Friars Road, Mission Valley; (619) 295–2087. Inexpensive.
Authentic Mexican cuisine, such as *mole* Polano, beef tongue Veracruz style, *carne asada* Tampiquena, breaded steak, and beef stew, accompanied by extralarge margaritas.

FIRST AVENUE
1055 First Avenue, San Diego; (619) 232–6141. Inexpensive to moderate.
A good place for steak—chopped, en brochette, rib eye, top sirloin, New York cut—as well as broiled swordfish and fried shrimp.

GELLEROSA RANCH BARBECUE
120 Ash Street, San Diego; (619) 232–2838. Inexpensive.
A wood-burning barbecue pit in downtown San Diego. This place uses a secret Oklahoma sauce to perk up the flavor of its ribs, chicken, and other meats. Features fresh strawberry-banana cake for dessert.

HOB NOB HILL
2271 First Avenue, San Diego, (619) 239–8176. Inexpensive to moderate.
This is San Diego's oldest family-owned restaurant and very popular with locals and visitors. Offers many selections and daily specials, plus homemade baked goodies.

JILLY'S RESTAURANT
515 Hawthorn Street, San Diego; (619) 544–0940. Moderate.

Cajun cooking, featuring blackened redfish, chicken jambalaya, catfish, and homemade hot chocolate pecan pie.

JOHN TARANTINO'S RESTAURANT
5150 North Harbor Drive, San Diego; (619) 224–3555. Moderate.
An excellent Italian restaurant that gives you a free cruise on Friday and Saturday nights while you wait for your table.

KAISERHOF RESTAURANT
5351 Adobe Falls Road, Mission Valley; (619) 287–3075. Moderate.
Traditional *wiener schnitzel mit rotkohl* (breaded veal cutlet with red cabbage), plus more German specialties and imported beers.

KOBE MISONO RESTAURANT
5451 Kearny Villa Road, San Diego; (619) 560–7399. Moderate.
A fine Japanese restaurant that features a sushi bar and hibachi cooking of seafood, beef, and chicken.

KUNG FOOD VEGETARIAN RESTAURANT
2949 Fifth Avenue, San Diego; (619) 298–7302. Inexpensive.
Kung Food offers delicious and creative vegetarian dishes. Many are low fat and salt free. The environment is relaxing, smoke free, and graced with candlelight and roses.

LAWRENCE WELK RESORT VILLAGE THEATRE
8860 Lawrence Welk Drive, Escondido; (619) 749–3448. Expensive.
The main course at this famous restaurant is prime roast beef, and the entertainment is popular music and comedy performed by professionals. If you are a Lawrence Welk fan, do not miss spending a memorable evening here.

OLD SPAGHETTI FACTORY
275 Fifth Avenue, San Diego; (619) 233–4323. Inexpensive.
A family restaurant located in the Gaslamp Quarter. Here kids and parents can fill up on several different kinds of pasta and pizza, as well as salads and desserts.

RAINWATER'S ON KETTNER
1202 Kettner Boulevard, San Diego; (619) 233–5757. Expensive.
The dining room overlooks the bay. Specialties include aged beef, aged steaks, and fresh seafood.

REUBEN E. LEE STERNWHEELER RESTAURANT
880 East Harbor Drive, San Diego; (619) 291–1870. Moderate.
Here you can feast on a ten-course meal on board a replica of an 1880s riverboat. Offers nice views of the city and harbor, plus live entertainment.

SHANGHAI RESTAURANT
4055 Fifty-fourth Street, San Diego; (619) 286–2345. Inexpensive.
A comprehensive menu of familiar and exotic Chinese dishes, including Mandarin cuisine and Mongolian barbecued beef and lamb.

SILAS ST. JOHN RESTAURANT
4720 Kensington Drive, San Diego; (619) 283–8343. Expensive.
An excellent French restaurant housed in a historic building, featuring complete, multicourse, fixed-price dinners and an extensive list of French and California wines. This is a no-smoking restaurant.

T. D. HAYS RESTAURANT
4315 Ocean Boulevard, San Diego; (619) 270–6505. Moderate to expensive.
A popular city seafood place located on the boardwalk. Highlighted are breads, turkey pot pies, croissants, and scrumptious desserts made fresh in their own bakery.

TOM HAM'S LIGHTHOUSE
2150 Harbor Island Drive, Harbor Island; (619) 291–9110. Moderate.
A restaurant overlooking the harbor and city skyline. Features steaks and fresh seafood, a soothing California decor, and live entertainment.

Entertainment

Greater San Diego presents a wealth of offerings when it comes to the performing arts and entertainment. For current information about entertainment in the area, call (619) 234–ARTS or (619) 295–WHIM. For available half-price tickets to various cultural and entertainment events, call Arts Tix at (619) 238–3810. In addition, *San Diego Magazine* contains detailed descriptions on performing arts and entertainment happenings while you are in town.

SAN DIEGO

OLD GLOBE THEATRE/SIMON EDISON CENTRE FOR THE PERFORMING ARTS

In Balboa Park, San Diego; box office (619) 239–2255.

The Old Globe is San Diego's Tony–Award winning resident professional theater company, well known for staging Shakespeare and the works of new playwrights. In 1988 it staged the world premiere of Neil Simon's *Jake's Women*. Among the famous actors who have appeared in Old Globe productions are Michael Learned, Marsha Mason, Christopher Reeve, Cliff Robertson, Christopher Walken, and Paul Winfield. Call for performance schedule and ticket availability before your visit to San Diego.

LA JOLLA PLAYHOUSE/MANDELL WEISS CENTER FOR THE PERFORMING ARTS

Corner of Torrey Pines Road and La Jolla Village Drive, La Jolla—about fifteen minutes north of downtown San Diego; box office (619) 534–3960.

La Jolla Playhouse was founded in 1947 by film stars Gregory Peck, Mel Ferrer, and Dorothy McGuire as a summer stock theater where movie actors could work their craft before live audiences. La Jolla Playhouse stages new and classical dramas and comedies from late May to early October.

San Diego Symphony, Symphony Hall at 1245 Seventh Avenue, San Diego; (619) 699–4205

San Diego Opera, Civic Theatre, 202 C Street, downtown San Diego; (619) 236–6510

San Diego Repertory Theatre, 79 Horton Plaza, downtown San Diego; (619) 235–8025

Gaslamp Quarter Theatre Company, 547 Fourth Avenue, Gaslamp Quarter of downtown San Diego; (619) 234–9583

Theatre in Old Town, 4040 Twiggs Street, Old Town section of San Diego; (619) 298–0082

San Diego Civic Light Opera Association, Starlight Bowl in Balboa Park, San Diego; (619) 544–7800

San Diego Gilbert and Sullivan Company, Casa del Prado Theatre in Balboa Park, San Diego; (619) 692–0372

Marie Hitchcock Puppet Theatre, Palisades Building in Balboa Park, San Diego; (619) 466–7128

ENTERTAINING PLACES

Some of the best places offering live entertainment and/or dancing are in hotels, such as at the San Diego Marriott, the Hotel del Coronado, and the U. S. Grant. Following is a tiny sample of the many bars and clubs that help to make visitors to the San Diego area happy.

The Comedy Store, 916 Pearl Street, La Jolla; (619) 454–9176
The Improv (comedy club), 832 Garnet Avenue, San Diego; (619) 483–4520
Lawrence Welk Village Theatre, 8860 Lawrence Welk Drive, Escondido; (619) 749–3448
Java Coffeehouse-Gallery, 837 G Street, downtown San Diego; (619) 235–4012
O'Hungry's (folk song place), 2547 San Diego Avenue, Old Town, San Diego; (619) 298–0133
B Street Cafe and Bar (jazz), 425 West B Street, downtown San Diego; (619) 236–1707

Shopping

A great array of wonderful specialty shops and department stores can be found throughout Greater San Diego. Horton Plaza in downtown is convenient for most visitors to the city. Other major shopping centers are Bazaar del Mundo on Juan Street in Old Town Historic Park, Stratford Square in Del Mar, La Jolla Village Square in La Jolla, and Mission Valley Center on Mission Center Road in San Diego. Seaport Village on the waterfront in downtown San Diego and the Old Ferry Landing across the harbor in Coronado are popular theme shopping and dining areas, offering the charming illusion of being in quaint coastal hamlets of a past time.

HORTON PLAZA
First and Fourth avenues, between Broadway and G streets; (619) 239–8180.

Horton Plaza is the heart of downtown San Diego. Here are several blocks of delights for shoppers, 4 major department stores, and 140 shops—Abercrombie and Fitch, Adventure 16 Wilderness Outfitters, B. Dalton Software, Bally of Switzerland, Banana Republic, Brentano's, Brookstone, Doubleday, Eddie Bauer, Foot Locker, Horton Toy and Doll, House of Almonds, Kite Country, Laura Ashley, Le Travel Store, The Nature Company, Nordstrom Department Store, Valley Sport, and Victoria's Secret. Horton Plaza also has cinemas, restaurants, cafes, Lyceum Theatres, and the San Diego Repertory

SAN DIEGO

Theater and offers numerous other entertainments, many of them free just for being there—dance bands during evenings, guitarists, flamenco dancers, jugglers, mimes, jazz musicians, and comics. Horton Plaza is esthetically beautiful in its architecture and landscaping. Just to be here at any time is to feel joy in an immensely human-focused city.

10

Greater Palm Springs: America's Capital of Resorts and Golf Courses

Greater Palm Springs is located in a desert valley lush with palm groves, lawns, and lakes. Flanking the valley are the Little San Bernardino Mountains, the San Bernardino Mountains, and the Santa Rosa Mountains. Here is one of America's most glamorous resort areas, home to such celebrities as former president Gerald Ford, Bob Hope, Frank Sinatra, Walter Annenberg, and Gene Autry. It is said that movie stars William Holden and Grace Kelly found romance together here; Marilyn Monroe was discovered at the Racquet Club; and Clark Gable and Carol Lombard honeymooned at the Ingleside Inn. The focus on fame, wealth, and physical beauty continues to inspire the Palm Springs scene.

The communities of Greater Palm Springs include Palm Springs, Rancho Mirage, La Quinta, Indian Wells, Cathedral City, Coachella, Desert Hot Springs, Bermuda Dunes, Indio, and Palm Desert.

In addition to its ideal climate, famous residents, and wonderful resorts, Greater Palm Springs is known throughout the world as a center for medicine. The Betty Ford Center, the Walter Annenberg Center for Health Science, the Hal Wallis Research Facility, the Barbara Sinatra Children's Center, and the Eisenhower Medical Center are here.

Here also are played some of America's top golf tournaments, such as the Bob Hope Chrysler Classic and the Dinah Shore Nabisco Invitational.

How to Get There

BY CAR

Palm Springs is 100 miles to the southeast of downtown Los Angeles, about a two-hour car ride on Interstate 10.

BY AIR

Several major national and regional airlines serve Palm Springs Regional Airport from Los Angeles, San Diego, Las Vegas, Denver, Dallas, Chicago, and many other cities. Consult your hometown travel agent about direct or connecting flights from your area or from other vacation destinations on your itinerary. Rental cars, limousines, shuttle services, and taxis are available at the airport.

How to Get Around

Palm Canyon Drive (Highway 111) is the main road that runs through most of the communities and provides access to resorts and attractions. Other main roads include Gene Autry Trail in Palm Springs, Gerald Ford and Bob Hope drives in Rancho Mirage, Country Club Drive in Rancho Mirage and Palm Desert, Fred Waring Drive in Palm Desert and Indian Wells, Dinah Shore Drive in Rancho Mirage, and Frank Sinatra Drive in Rancho Mirage; these are located between Highway 111 on the west and Interstate 10 on the east. Highway 74 off of Highway 111 in Palm Desert leads to the Pacific Coast and San Diego. Interstate 10 goes east to Phoenix, Arizona.

These companies provide sightseeing, special interest, and executive tours:

American Travel Planners, (619) 341–7778
Brier-Kushner Associates, (619) 568–3439
California Leisure Consultants, (619) 323–7728
Celebrity Tours of Palm Springs, (619) 325–2682
Creations Unlimited, (619) 320–2095
Desert Caravans, (619) 568–0608
Gadabout Tours, (619) 323–5556
Gray Line Tours, (619) 325–0974
Lost Penguin Tours, (619) 329–4546
Palm Springs Safari and Executive Tours, (619) 320–4664
Safaris, (619) 341–3761

Tourism Information

Greater Palm Springs Convention and Visitors Bureau, Airport Park Plaza, #315, 225 North El Cielo Road, Palm Springs; (619) 327–8411.
Rancho Mirage Chamber of Commerce, 42-464 The Veldt, Rancho Mirage; (619) 568–9351.
Greater Palm Springs Twenty-four-hour Activity Hotline, (619) 322–4636

Important Telephone Numbers

Emergencies (Police, Fire, Medical), Dial 911
California Highway Patrol, dial Operator and ask for ZENITH 1–2000
Road Conditions, (619) 345–2767
Weather, (619) 345–3711
Eisenhower Medical Center, (619) 340–3911
Twenty-four-hour Dental Emergency, (619) 327–8448

Special Events

The following are significant special events that take place in Greater Palm Springs during the peak vacation season, from November through March. For a complete list of special events (sports, performing arts, shows, exhibitions, etc.) or more information on those listed here, call the **Greater Palm Springs Convention and Visitors Bureau** at (619) 327–8411. *Palm Springs Life* magazine, available at all newsstands and at hotels, also publishes current listings of special events and entertainment offerings in its *Desert Guide* monthly.

NOVEMBER
Annual Red Cross Golf Tournament, Indian Wells, early November
Wilson/PGA Professional Golf Classic, La Quinta, early November
Annual Palm Springs Vintage Grand Prix Auto Race, Palm Springs, mid- to late November
Nordic Ski Center reopens at the top of Palm Springs Aerial Tramway, mid-November

Annual Tram Road Challenge (a tough 6K run up the lower slope of the mountain), Palm Springs, late November

Skins Golf Game (PGA top players), La Quinta, late November

DECEMBER

Annual Billy Barty Golf Classic, Palm Springs, early December

Poinsettia Ball, Rancho Mirage, early December

World Pro-Am Golf Championship, La Quinta, mid-December

Annual Village Center for the Arts, Palm Springs, mid-December

JANUARY

Annual National Collegiate Tennis Classic, Palm Desert, early January

Bob Hope Chrysler Golf Classic, Palm Desert, early January

Moosehead Sled Dog Classic, top of Palm Springs Aerial Tramway, mid-January

Adidas Invitational Tennis Tournament, Indian Wells, late January

FEBRUARY

Frank Sinatra Invitational Golf Tournament, Palm Springs, early February

Annual Antique Show, Palm Springs, mid-February

Annual National Date Festival, Indio, mid-February

Southern California Invitational Senior Olympics, Palm Springs, late February to early March

MARCH

PGA Legends of Golf Tournament, Indian Wells, March

Annual Square and Round Dance Festival, Palm Springs, early March

Annual La Quinta Arts Festival, La Quinta, early March

Newsweek Champions Tennis Cup Matches, Indian Wells, mid-March

Nabisco Dinah Shore Golf Classic, Mission Hills, late March to early April

America's Capital of Golf

Within Coachella Valley are some of the world's most challenging and beautiful golf courses. The following list of golf courses is organized by the communities in which they are located. These courses are open to play by the general public and so are designated **public. Reciprocal** is another designation used here; it means that the course is private but has reciprocal arrangements with golf courses throughout North America and in other countries. If you belong to a country club or have membership at a golf course, you can play reciprocal courses. Be sure to call the course of your choice ahead of time to make arrangements for play.

In addition to the listed courses, there are a number of strictly private ones, not listed here, where members are allowed to bring guests for play.

CATHEDRAL CITY
Cathedral Canyon Country Club, Cathedral Canyon Drive; (619) 328–6571. Reciprocal, 18 holes, par 72; tennis courts.
De Anza-Palm Spring Country Club, Date Palm Drive; (619) 328–1315. Public, 18 holes, par 58; tennis courts.
Desert Princess Country Club, Landau Way; (619) 322–2280. Reciprocal, 18 holes, par 72; tennis courts.

DESERT HOT SPRINGS
Desert Crest Country Club, Desert Crest Avenue; (619) 329–8711. Public, 9 holes, par 27.
Mission Lakes Country Club, Clubhouse Boulevard; (619) 329–8061. Public, 18 holes, par 71; tennis courts.
Sands Mobile Home Country Club, Bubbling Wells Road; (619) 329–8816. Public, 9 holes, par 29.
Sands RV Country Club, Bubbling Wells Road; (619) 251–1173. Public, 9 holes, par 32.

INDIAN WELLS
Indian Wells Country Club, Club Drive; (619) 345–2561. Reciprocal, 27 holes, par 72.
Indian Wells Golf Resort, Indian Wells Lane; (619) 346–4653. Public, 36 holes, par 72; tennis courts.

INDIO
Indian Palms Country Club, Monroe Way; (619) 347–2326. Public, 27 holes, par 72; tennis courts.
Indian Springs Country Club, Jefferson Street; (619) 345–2838. Public, 18 holes, par 71.
Indio Municipal Golf Course, Avenue 42; (619) 347–9156. Public, 18 holes, par 54.

PALM SPRINGS

LA QUINTA
La Quinta Hotel Citrus Course, Jefferson Street; (619) 564–7620. Public, 18 holes, par 72.
La Quinta Hotel Dunes Course, Avenue Vista Bonita; (619) 345–2549. Public, 18 holes, par 72; tennis courts.
Palm Royale Country Club, Fred Waring at Washington; (619) 345–9701. Public, 18 holes, a par 3 course; tennis courts.
PGA West Resort Courses Course, PGA Boulevard; (619) 564–7170. Public, 36 holes, par 71; tennis courts.

PALM DESERT
Avondale Golf Course, Avondale Drive; (619) 345–3712. Reciprocal, 18 holes, par 72; tennis courts.
Chaparral Country Club, Chaparral Drive; (619) 340–1501. Reciprocal, 18 holes, par 60/62; tennis courts.
Desert Falls Country Club, Desert Falls Parkway; (619) 341–4020. Public, 18 holes, par 72.
Marrakesh Golf Course, Marrakesh Drive; (619) 568–2660. Reciprocal, 18 holes, par 60; tennis courts.
Marriott's Desert Springs Resort Palm Course, Country Club Drive; (619) 341–1756. Public, 36 holes, par 72; tennis courts.
Monterey Country Club, Monterey Avenue; (619) 346–1115. Reciprocal, 27 holes, par 72/71; tennis courts.
Oasis Country Club, Casbah Way; (619) 345–2715. Public, 18 holes, par 60; tennis courts.
Palm Desert Country Club, California Way; (619) 345–2525. Public, 27 holes, par 72/34; tennis courts.
Palm Desert Resort Country Club, Country Club Drive; (619) 345–2791. Public, 18 holes, par 72; tennis courts.
Palm Valley Country Club, Country Club Drive; (619) 345-2742. Reciprocal, 27 holes, par 72.
Shadow Mountain Golf Club, Portola Way; (619) 568–5717. Reciprocal, 18 holes, par 69.
Suncrest Country Club, Country Club Drive; (619) 340–2467. Public, 9 holes, par 66; tennis courts.
Woodhaven Country Club, Woodhaven Drive; (619) 345–7513. Reciprocal, 18 holes, par 70; tennis courts.

PALM SPRINGS
Canyon South Golf Course, Murray Canyon Drive; (619) 327–2019. Public, 18 holes, par 71.

Marriott's Desert Springs Resort & Spa, near Palm Springs, features a 100-foot-high atrium lobby with many plants, two waterfalls, and an indoor lake.

Fairchild's Bel Aire Greens, South El Cielo Road; (619) 327–0332. Public, 9 holes, par 32.
Mesquite Country Club, East Mesquite Avenue; (619) 323–1502. Public, 18 holes, par 72.
O'Donnell Golf Club, North Belardo Road; (619) 325–2259. Reciprocal, 9 holes, par 72.
Palm Springs Country Club, Whitewater Club Drive; (619) 323–2626. Public, 18 holes, par 72; tennis courts.
Palm Springs Municipal Golf Course, Golf Club Drive; (619) 328–1005. Public, 18 holes, par 72.

RANCHO MIRAGE
Marriott's Rancho Las Palmas Country Club, Bob Hope Drive; (619) 568–0955. Reciprocal, 27 holes, par 70/71/69; tennis courts.
Mission Hills Resort Golf Club, Dinah Shore Drive; (619) 328–3198. Public, 54 holes, par 72; tennis courts.
Rancho Mirage Country Club, Bob Hope Drive; (619) 324–4711. Reciprocal, 18 holes, par 70; tennis courts.
Sunrise Country Club, Country Club Drive; (619) 328–1139. Reciprocal, 18 holes, par 64; tennis courts.

THOUSAND PALMS
Ivey Ranch Country Club, Varner Road; (619) 343–2013. Public, 9 holes, par 68; tennis court.

Other Sports and Recreational Activities

BIKING
Bike-trail maps are available at the City of Palm Springs Recreation Department. The **Palm Springs Cycle Sports Club** offers tours throughout the valley; call (619) 340–2840 or 325–9319 for more information. These organizations provide bike rentals:

Burnett's Bicycle Barn, Palm Springs, (619) 325–7844
Canyon Bicycle Rentals and Tours, Palm Springs, (619) 327–7688
Mac's Bike Rentals, Palm Springs, (619) 327–5721

POLO
Eldorado Polo Club, Indio; (619) 342–2223. Plays from November to April.

PALM SPRINGS

HELICOPTER TOURING
HeleAir, Palm Springs; (619) 344–4321
Landells Aviation, Desert Hot Springs; (619) 329–6468

HIKING
The Palm Springs Leisure Center offers field trips every Wednesday, November through April, with a Palm Springs Desert Museum naturalist; call (619) 325–7186 for information. The Tahquitz Group of the San Gorgonio chapter of the Sierra Club has weekend hikes in the Coachella Valley and mountains; for information, call (619) 346–6798.

HORSEBACK RIDING
Smoke Tree Stables, Palm Springs; (619) 327–1372
Vandenberg Stables, Palm Springs; (619) 328–4560

HOT AIR BALLOONING
Desert Balloon Charters, Palm Desert; (619) 346–8575
Fantasy Balloon Flights, Palm Springs; (619) 568–0997
Rise and Float Balloon Tours, Palm Springs; (619) 341–2686
Sunrise Balloons, Thermal; (619) 346–7591

ICE SKATING
Ice Capades Chalet, in Palm Desert Town Center, is an attractive year-round rink. Ice Capades stars make celebrity appearances; classes available for all ages. Call (619) 340–4412 for information.

FISHING AND BOATING
Fishing and boating is available at Lake Cahilla in Indio (714–787–2553) and at Lake Hemet near Idyllwild.

TRAP AND SKEET SHOOTING
Palm Springs Regional Trap & Skeet Club, Indio; (619) 347–4811

PUBLIC TENNIS COURTS
The Tennis Center, Palm Springs; (619) 320–0020

SWIMMING
Most places of accommodation have swimming pools and spas (Jacuzzi, whirlpool, sauna, etc.).

ULTRALIGHT AIRCRAFT FLIGHTS
Oasis Ultralight Flight Park, Bermuda Dunes; (619) 345–7460

Attractions

PALM SPRINGS AERIAL TRAMWAY/MOUNT SAN JACINTO STATE WILDERNESS
Located on Highway 111 and Tramway Road; (619) 325–1449. Admission charge. Open all year, except for two weeks after Labor Day when the facility is closed for maintenance.

Here is one of California's great scenic experiences. An eighty-passenger tramcar carries you from the warm desert up to bracing alpine air at Mountain Station, at an elevation of 8,516 feet. This thrilling yet safe ride takes about eighteen minutes. Once on top, you have magnificent views of the desert below and of surrounding wilderness areas. You are also within the 13,000-acre San Jacinto State Park, with its 54 miles of hiking and backpacking trails.

During the summer a wilderness trail ride and nature hikes are offered; in winter, cross-country skiing, with equipment rentals and instruction available at the Nordic Ski Center (the center operates from about November 15 to April 15). There are picnic areas, eleven campgrounds, and lookout places with telescopes. At Mountain Station there are a restaurant, a lounge, and a gift shop. Permits are required for hiking, backpacking, and camping. No smoking is allowed on trails; no fires are allowed; all flora and fauna are protected and cannot be removed; hikers must stay on trails; and campers under eighteen must be accompanied by an adult.

BIG MORONGO WILDLIFE RESERVE—COVINGTON PARK
Interstate 10 to Highway 62 to East Drive. Free. Open daily, 8:00 A.M. to sunset.

In the past, Big Morongo was an Indian village and later a cattle ranch. It is now a regional park containing three hundred species of plants and is also a well-known wildlife sanctuary and birding area. There is good hiking in the park.

COACHELLA VALLEY MUSEUM AND CULTURAL CENTER
81-616 Miles Avenue, Indio; (619) 342–6651. Admission charge. Open Tuesday through Saturday from 10:00 A.M. to 4:00 P.M. and Sunday from noon to 4:00 P.M.

The works of Palm Springs area artists and craftspeople are displayed at the center. A permanent collection of historic artifacts are exhibited in an adobe building.

COACHELLA VALLEY PRESERVE
Located 10 miles east of Palm Springs near Thousand Palms, via Interstate 10 to Ramon Road; (619) 343–1234. Free. Open daily from sunrise to sunset.

This 13,000-acre nature preserve contains a varied desert ecosystem that includes the Thousand Palms oasis, clear streams, mesas, sand dunes, and buffs. It is rich in animal and bird life. The preserve is open to hiking and horseback trail riding. Coachella Valley Preserve is owned and operated by the Nature Conservancy, the Bureau of Land Management, the U.S. Fish and Wildlife Service, and the California Department of Fish and Game.

DATE GARDENS
The greater Palm Springs area calls itself the Date Capital of the World. Here many different kinds of dates are grown, packed, and shipped to customers all over the world. These date gardens welcome visitors: Oasis Date Gardens in Thermal, Indian Wells Date Gardens in Palm Desert, and Shields Date Gardens on Highway 111 near Indio. The Desert Date Shop in Palm Springs sells date milk shakes and chocolate-covered dates.

INDIAN CANYONS
South Palm Canyon Drive, Palm Springs; (619) 325–5673. Admission charge. Open daily from September to June, 8:30 A. M. to 5:00 P.M.

This very scenic area in the Andreas, Murray, and Palm canyons is perfect for hiking, picnicking, and horseback trail riding. An Indian trading post is also here.

JOSHUA TREE NATIONAL MONUMENT
Headquarters at Twenty-nine Palms, via Interstate 10 and Highway 62 through Morongo and Yucca Valley; (619) 367–7511. Admission charge per car. Open throughout the year.

Joshua Tree is a huge wildlife sanctuary, consisting of more than 870 square miles. It is rich in wildlife, birds, and flora, such as the Joshua tree, the tall, branched yucca plant from which it takes its name. The park has eight campgrounds, as well as hiking and horseback trails.

PALM SPRINGS

KINGDOM OF THE DOLLS

66071 Pierson Boulevard, Desert Hot Springs; (619) 329–5137. Admission charge. Open Tuesday through Sunday, noon to 6:00 P.M.

A special museum that contains hundreds of dolls dressed in costumes representing different periods in human history. Betty Hamilton, born in Denmark, created this unique world of dolls over eighteen years of dedicated labor.

LIVING DESERT

47-900 Portola Drive, Palm Desert; (619) 346–5694; Admission charge. Open daily, 9:00 A.M. to 5:00 P.M.; closed June through August.

Living Desert features 1,200 acres of natural history experiences for visitors—for example, exhibits of desert mammals and reptiles, geological displays, and botanical gardens—and has several miles of nature trails and areas for picnics. The H. Earl Hoover Education Center offers educational programs on the wildlife, birding, and ecology of the desert.

MCCALLUM ADOBE

221 South Canyon Drive, Palm Springs; (619) 323–8297. Admission charge. Open Wednesday through Sunday from noon to 3:00 P.M. (Thursday and Saturday, 10:00 A.M. to 4:00 P.M.); closed June to mid-October.

This adobe dwelling, constructed in 1885, served as home for the John Gutherie McCallum family, pioneers in the valley. It now belongs to the Palm Springs Historical Society.

MOORTEN BOTANICAL GARDEN

1701 South Palm Canyon Drive, Palm Springs; (619) 327–6555. Admission charge. Open daily, 9:00 A.M. to 5:00 P.M.

A world-famous desert garden displaying two thousand varieties of cacti, succulents, trees, flowers, and birds. Nature trails show visitors that the desert is not a barren place but rich in many forms of life unique to its ecology.

OASIS WATER RESORT

1500 Gene Autry Trail, Palm Springs; (619) 325–SURF. Admission charge. Open daily from March to September, 11:00 A.M. to 5:00 P.M.

A family water theme park featuring a 29,000-square-foot wave pool that whips up 3- to 4-foot-high waves for bodysurfing. The attraction also has Hydrotwist speed slides, Typhoon free-fall slides, thrill flumes, and a white-water river, as well as spas, volleyball courts, swimming pools, and other recreational facilities.

PALM SPRINGS DESERT MUSEUM

101 Museum Drive, Palm Springs; (619) 325–7186. Admission charge. Open Tuesday through Friday from 10:00 A.M. to 4:00 P.M. and Saturday and Sunday from 10:00 A.M. to 5:00 P.M.

This exceptional natural science complex has several galleries of exhibits, a theater for the performing arts, a sunken sculpture garden, displays of Indian artifacts, and arts-and-crafts exhibitions. The museum also sponsors lectures and field trips.

PIONEERTOWN

Via Highway 62 to Yucca Valley. Open all year.

Pioneertown was built in the 1940s by cowboy film stars Roy Rogers and Gene Autry as an old-time western town for motion picture and television production. This is not a western ghost town but a community of people who provide visitors with western-style entertainment and covered-wagon rides. Pioneertown also has a campground, an art gallery, a bowling alley, and a restaurant.

Resort Accommodations

The communities of Greater Palm Springs contain a fabulous collection of luxury resorts. Although this is desert country, each one of those resorts is an attractive garden oasis of lawns, trees, flower beds, and water areas—some of the most beautiful landscaping found anywhere. Many resorts are remarkable architectural complexes that would make the grand palaces in the *Arabian Nights* seem shabby by comparison. Most offer superbly furnished rooms with modern comforts and amenities and feature gourmet restaurants and cocktail lounges with live entertainment. Many have golf courses, swimming pools, tennis, bike rentals, health and fitness facilities, shops, and much more.

When it is icy elsewhere in North America, Greater Palm Springs is in its peak season. It is a period when resorts charge top rates. Summer is a slower time but also less costly. To receive the best value, contact your hometown travel agent for a vacation package. For more information on resort accommodations, call the **Greater Palm Springs Convention and Visitors Bureau** at (619) 327–8411.

DOUBLETREE RESORT AT DESERT PRINCESS COUNTRY CLUB

Vista Chino and Landau Boulevard, Palm Springs; (619) 322-7000 or (800) 344-2626. Expensive.

A large, modern resort complex offering fine accommodations, including two-bedroom condos overlooking its eighteen-hole golf course. Featured also are ten tennis courts, two racquetball courts, a swimming pool, dining at the Princess Restaurant, and dancing and live entertainment at the Oasis.

FOUR SEASONS APARTMENT HOTEL

290 San Jacinto Drive, Palm Springs; (619) 325-6427. Moderate to expensive.

Luxury accommodations on an expertly landscaped site. Offers a swimming pool, whirlpool, bikes, and some units with kitchens.

GENE AUTRY HOTEL

4200 East Palm Canyon Drive, Palm Springs; (619) 328-1171 or (800) 443-6328. Expensive.

An excellent luxury hotel on oasislike grounds. Named after the famous cowboy of the movies, the hotel offers rooms with patios or balconies, three swimming pools, several tennis courts, a restaurant, and a lounge with entertainment.

HYATT GRAND CHAMPIONS RESORT

Indian Wells Lane, Indian Wells; (619) 325-5972 or (800) 228-9000. Expensive.

A superior resort on beautifully landscaped grounds, offering first-rate rooms and dining places, a lounge, a swimming pool, and golf, tennis, and health and fitness facilities.

INDIAN WELLS RACQUET CLUB RESORT

46-765 Bay Club Drive, Indian Wells; (619) 345-2811. Moderate to expensive.

Located near the Santa Rosa Mountains about twenty minutes from downtown. Prime accommodations in a garden oasis setting. Offers ten championship tennis courts, a golf course, four swimming pools, fine dining, and many other guest amenities.

INGLESIDE INN

200 West Ramon Road at Belardo, Palm Springs; (619) 325-0046 or (800) 772-6655. Moderate to expensive.

A favorite with movie stars and pop entertainers, Ingleside is a small inn with much charm. It is decorated with antiques and offers a swimming pool and other recreations. Its Melvyn's Restaurant serves chateaubriand *bouquetiere,* Milanese scampi, fresh Norwegian salmon with hollandaise, and other delicious dishes.

LA MANCHA PRIVATE VILLAS AND COURT CLUB

444 North Avenida Caballeros, Palm Springs; (619) 323–1773. Expensive.

Large, nicely furnished rooms, suites, and villas; many villas have private patios and fireplaces. Offers a swimming pool, a putting green, tennis courts, bike rentals, an exercise room, a restaurant, and a cocktail lounge.

LA QUINTA HOTEL GOLF AND TENNIS RESORT

49-499 Eisenhower Drive, La Quinta; (619) 564–4111 or (800) 854–1271. Moderate to expensive.

This lovely resort has seen the likes of Clark Gable, Greta Garbo, Gloria Swanson, Errol Flynn, and many other stars. It offers thirty tennis courts (grass, hard, and Har-Tu clay), thirty-six holes of championship golf, a swimming pool, and numerous guest amenities; golf and tennis packages are available. Accommodations and dining are excellent, and there are dancing and live entertainment in the Santa Rosa Room. La Quinta recently completed a $45 million expansion, making it one of the most complete and most beautiful resorts in the valley.

MARRIOTT'S DESERT SPRINGS RESORT & SPA

74855 Country Club Drive, Palm Desert; (619) 341–2211 or (800) 228-9290. Expensive.

This gorgeous resort and spa offers luxurious vacations in a lush oasis setting. Covering 400 acres, 23 of them lakes and waterways, Marriott's Desert Springs features two eighteen-hole golf courses designed by Ted Robinson; sixteen tennis courts, seven of which are illuminated for night play; three swimming pools; ten restaurants and lounges; a shopping arcade; entertainment; a health and fitness spa; and a beauty salon.

The resort's extensive health and fitness facilities include exercise equipment, aerobics classes, yoga, walking and jogging paths, Swiss showers and steam rooms, and various body treatments such as massages and herbal wraps. The spa provides special package plans of supervised programs for those who want to beat fatigue, get in shape, and look and feel good. Facial treatments are provided by Kerstin Florian, a well-known Swedish skin-care expert. Jose Eber, of swanky Rodeo Drive in Los Angeles, operates the beauty salon.

Tastefully furnished guest rooms feature a minibar, a balcony with great views of the San Jacinto Mountains, and many other fine guest amenities. The resort has restaurants for every taste—Lake View for California food, Sea Grille for fresh seafood, and Mikado for Japanese Teppan-yaki cooking.

MARRIOTT'S RANCHO LAS PALMAS

41000 Bob Hope Drive, Rancho Mirage; (619) 568–2727 or (800) 228–9290. Expensive.

This superb resort—early California hacienda style—offers spacious rooms with a balcony or patio overlooking enticing grounds, twenty-seven holes of golf with complete country club privileges, twenty-five tennis courts, and three swimming pools. Continental cuisine is served at Cabrillo and family-style meals at Fountain Court; dancing and live entertainment are offered at Miguel's. *Mobil Travel Guide* gave Rancho Las Palmas its rare five-star award for excellence.

MAXIM'S DE PARIS SUITE HOTEL

285 North Palm Canyon Drive, Palm Springs; (619) 322–9000 or (800) 562–9467. Expensive.

Deluxe suites with balconies, plus a swimming pool, a sauna, an exercise room, a restaurant, and a lounge with entertainment.

MISSION HILLS RESORT HOTEL

71333 Dinah Shore Drive, Rancho Mirage; (619) 328–5955 or (800) 843–8988. Expensive.

A premium luxury resort for golfers and leisure seekers, offering fine accommodations and dining, an eighteen-hole championship golf course, swimming pools and spas, a tennis center, and many other choice guest amenities. Truffles is the hotel's elegant restaurant.

OASIS WATER RESORT VILLA HOTEL

2345 Cherokee Way, Palm Springs; (619) 328–1499 or (800) 543–5160. Expensive.

A deluxe resort and water park, containing twenty-one acres of swimming pools, water slides, beach cabanas, a sand beach, a wave-action pool, and volleyball courts. Offers a European-style health and fitness club with a spring-loaded aerobics floor, indoor racquetball courts, tennis courts (grass and clay), separate adult and children zones, and units with kitchens and dining areas.

PALM SPRINGS PLAZA RESORT AND RACQUET CLUB
400 East Tahquitz Way, Palm Springs; (619) 320–6868. Moderate to expensive.
World-class accommodations with balconies or patios. The resort features a swimming pool, tennis courts, a whirlpool and sauna, a health spa, a restaurant, and a lounge with entertainment.

PALM SPRINGS RIVIERA HOTEL RESORT AND CONVENTION CENTER
1600 North Indian Avenue, Palm Springs; (619) 327–8311. Expensive.
A large resort hotel offering good rooms, a restaurant and lounge, tennis, a swimming pool, and many other guest amenities.

RACQUET CLUB OF PALM SPRINGS
2743 North Indian Avenue, Palm Springs; (619) 325–1281. Expensive.
Fine resort accommodations and amenities, including tennis, a swimming pool and spa, a restaurant, and a lounge.

RITZ CARLTON RANCHO MIRAGE
68-900 Frank Sinatra Drive, Rancho Mirage; (619) 321–8282 or (800) 341–3333. Expensive.
A beautiful, secluded resort offering ten tennis courts, a fitness center, a swimming pool, and a Jacuzzi overlooking the valley and desert landscape. Features fine dining and comfortable accommodations. Championship golf courses, shops, and restaurants are nearby.

STOUFFER INDIAN WELLS RESORT
Highway 111, Palm Desert; (619) 773–4444. Expensive.
A luxury resort offering fine accommodations and dining, together with golf, tennis, a swimming pool, a health and fitness facility, a restaurant, a lounge, and many other guest amenities.

WYNDHAM PALM SPRINGS
888 East Tahquitz Way, Palm Springs; (619) 322–6000 or (800) 872–4335. Expensive.

A sumptuous hotel in a lovely garden setting. This Wyndham offers excellent accommodations, a health club, a swimming pool, dining at Cafe Jardin and Appley's, cocktails, and dancing at Situations. The hotel is near the chic shops on Palm Canyon Drive, golf courses, and other attractions.

OTHER RECOMMENDED ACCOMMODATIONS

Cathedral Canyon Resort, 34-567 Cathedral Canyon Drive, Palm Springs; (619) 321–9000. Moderate to expensive.

Embassy Suites Resort, 74-700 Highway 111, Palm Desert; (619) 340–6600 or (800) EMBASSY. Expensive.

Indian Wells Ramada, 76-661 Highway 111, Indian Wells; (619) 345–6466 or (800) 2–RAMADA. Moderate to expensive.

Marriott Courtyard, 1300 Tahquits Way, Palm Springs; (800) 321–2211. Moderate.

Palm Springs Marquis, 150 South Indian Avenue, Palm Springs; (619) 322–2121. (800) 458–6679. Expensive.

Palm Springs Resort Hotel and Villas, 2800 South Palm Canyon Drive, Palm Springs; (619) 327–3744 or (800) 522–5550. Expensive.

Palm Valley Country Club, 76-300 Country Club Drive, Palm Desert; (619) 345–5695. Moderate to expensive.

Radisson Palms Springs Resort, 1600 North Indian Avenue, Palm Springs; (619) 327–8311. Expensive.

Shadow Mountain Resort and Racquet Club, 45-750 San Luis Rey, Palm Desert; (619) 346–6123 or (800) 472–3713. Expensive.

Spa Hotel and Mineral Springs, 100 North Indian Avenue, Palm Springs; (619) 325–1461 or (800) 854–1279. Expensive.

Dining

The restaurants and resort dining rooms of Greater Palm Springs make those who are famished for fantastic food believe they are in gourmet heaven. The Italian restaurants here, for example, are exceptional, with many serving osso buco (tender veal shank in savory sauce) and calamari (delicious squid). There are also fine French, Chinese, and Mexican restaurants. With such an affluent crowd residing in and flowing in and out of valley communities, the deluxe continental restaurants have to keep on their toes to please palates used to the best. The following nonresort restaurants are recommended.

BEACH HOUSE INN
70-115 Highway 111, Rancho Mirage; (619) 328–6585. Moderate to expensive.
The ambience is Cape Cod in the desert. The Beach House Inn has more than twenty selections of seafood and meat dishes. There is also an oyster bar.

CEDAR CREEK INN
1555 South Palm Canyon Drive, Palm Springs; (619) 325–7300. Moderate.
A country inn atmosphere and decor and a comfortable place for homemade soups, meat or seafood entrees, and lip-smacking desserts.

DAR MAGHREB RESTAURANT
42-300 Bob Hope Drive, Rancho Mirage; (619) 568–9486. Moderate.
What better place to enjoy the food of Morocco than in the desert oasis of Palm Springs? Dar Maghreb presents a many-course feast in an exotic environment.

DIAMICO'S STEAK HOUSE
1180 South Palm Canyon Drive, Palm Springs; (619) 325–9191. Moderate.
Great beef and steak dishes, plus fresh seafood and such specialties as liver steak vaquero, son-of-a-gun stew, and the original Martiniburger. Entertainment in the lounge.

DOMINICK'S
70-30 Highway 111, Rancho Mirage; (619) 324–1711. Moderate to expensive.
A beautiful dining room in which fine beef, veal, seafood, and Italian dishes are served.

DON DIEGO'S
74-969 Highway 111, Indian Wells; (619) 340–5588. Inexpensive to moderate.
An award-winning Mexican restaurant. Favorite dishes include tamales, *fajitas,* and *chilis rellenos* Mazatlán. Huge margaritas.

FAIRCHILD'S
1001 El Cielo Road, Palm Springs; (619) 327–1263. Expensive.

A top continental cuisine restaurant with excellent service. The dining room overlooks the lake at Bel Air Greens. Entrees include prime beef, tender veal, and fresh seafood dishes.

FLOWER DRUM

424 South Indian Avenue, Palm Springs; (619) 323–3020. Inexpensive to moderate.

This fine restaurant offers the five regional cuisines of China—Szechwan, Peking, Shanghai, Hunan, and Canton. The chefs here do not use MSG. Low-sodium soy sauce, corn oil, and brown rice are used in the cooking.

HOUSE OF SENSU

169 North Indian Avenue, Palm Springs; (619) 322–0090. Moderate to expensive.

No-MSG Japanese cooking. House of Sensu offers Nigiri sushi, Maki sushi, sashimi, and boat dinners, as well as sukiyaki dinners cooked at your table. For dessert, try the deep-fried ice cream.

KIYOSAKU RESTAURANT

456 North Palm Canyon Drive, Palm Springs; (619) 327–6601. Moderate to expensive.

The city's authentic Japanese restaurant, offering sashimi, tempura, sukiyaki, and a unique boat dinner of beef and chicken teriyaki on a skewer, accompanied by shrimp, tempura vegetables, and fruit. You can also dine on *Kiyosaku-nabe*, which is a Japanese bouillabaisse (a thick fish soup).

LA MANCHA

444 Avenida Caballeros, Palm Springs; (619) 323–1773. Expensive.

One of the specialties of this superior restaurant is "Eye of the Rack" lamb prepared with Perigeux. If you wish a rare-vintage Chateau Lafite Rothschild rouge to go along with the lamb, La Mancha has it, as well as many other hard-to-find premium wines.

LAS CASUELAS-THE ORIGINAL

368 North Palm Canyon Drive, Palm Springs; (619) 325–3213. Inexpensive to moderate.

A popular Mexican restaurant. The menu has many enticing selections to mull over while you sip the giant margaritas.

LE PAON
45-640 Highway 74, Palm Desert; (619) 568–3651. Expensive.

An elegant French restaurant that features at-your-table preparation of steak Diane and crepes suzette. Candlelight dining; entertainment at night.

LE VALLAURIS
385 West Tahquitz Way, Palm Springs; (619) 325–5059. Expensive.

A highly honored French restaurant providing excellent food and service in a comfortable environment. Le Vallauris is a top choice for those who want the best.

LORD FLETCHER INN
70-385 Highway 111, Rancho Mirage; (619) 328–1161. Moderate to expensive.

Provides the warm charm and welcome of an English country inn. The well-prepared entrees include traditional roast beef and fresh seafood.

MANCUSO'S TRATTORIA
73-520 El Paseo Drive, Palm Desert; (619) 346–0445. Expensive.

An elegant place offering classic northern Italian dishes. The trattoria's specialty is osso buco. Dover sole, filet mignon, and fresh seafood also highlight the menu.

NATE'S DELICATESSEN AND RESTAURANT
100 South Indian Avenue, Palm Springs; (619) 325–3506. Inexpensive to moderate.

Nate is known hereabouts as Mr. Corned Beef of Palm Springs, which means his sandwiches make you want to sing with joy. Nate also makes a lot of other good things to eat. He has, for example, a cocktail called Borscht on the Rocks.

RICCIO'S
2155 North Palm Canyon Drive, Palm Springs; (619) 325–2369. Expensive.

Gourmet Italian cuisine and attentive service. Features homemade pastas and delicious veal and provides crystal and silver place settings. Well worth the time and money.

RISTORANTE MAMMA GINA

73-705 El Paseo Drive, Palm Desert; (619) 568–9898. Moderate to expensive.

Northern Italian food that is exceptional. Specialties include Tuscan antipasto, osso buco alla Florentino, and irresistible Florentine desserts.

SCOMA'S OF SAN FRANCISCO

69-629 Highway 111, Rancho Mirage; (619) 328–9000. Moderate to expensive.

This is the Palm Springs branch of a well-known San Francisco Fisherman's Wharf restaurant. The extensive seafood menu includes calamari, dore (white fish), sautéed shellfish, and veal and beef entrees.

SIAMESE GOURMET

4711 East Canyon Drive, Palm Springs; (619) 328–0057. Inexpensive to moderate.

The traditional cuisine of Thailand is lovingly prepared and served here. A nice alternative to the usual.

A TOUCH OF MAMA'S

74-063 Highway 111, Palm Desert; (619) 568–1315. Moderate.

Good, hearty Italian food prepared by Mama herself, Jovanna Carlton Cruz. Offered are osso buco, duck, Cornish hen, calamari marinara, homemade pasta, and more tummy- and soul-satisfying foods.

WILDE GOOSE

67-938 East Palm Canyon Drive, Cathedral City; (619) 328–5775. Moderate to expensive.

Food for gourmets—beef Wellington, lobster in cognac sauce, several kinds of duck dishes, wild game entrees, fresh seafood, and superb desserts.

WOODY'S CLASSIC COOKHOUSE

Palm Desert Town Center, Palm Desert; (619) 341–4335. Inexpensive to moderate.

Whopping burgers and sandwiches, along with salads, ribs, steaks, *fajitas,* and chicken. A zany, humorous decor.

Entertainment

Some of the superlative entertainment offerings in Greater Palm Springs are found in the clubs, lounges, and dining rooms of the august resorts and at many restaurants. Both established stars and new talents play Palm Springs. This is the place for the big names to perform before friends and for unknowns with star quality to be discovered. The valley is that powerful a draw for entertainers, which means you get to see and enjoy the best. For information on current events, call the Greater Palm Springs Twenty-Four-Hour Activity Hotline at (619) 322–4636. In addition, your hotel concierge or guest relations person will provide you with more information and can obtain tickets. A listing of current entertainments is also published in the monthly **Palm Springs Life** magazine, available at valley newsstands and resorts.

THE BOB HOPE CULTURAL CENTER
73-000 Fred Waring Drive, Palm Desert; (619) 340–ARTS.
   On January 2, 1988, the Bob Hope Cultural Center made its debut. The glittering opening was abundant with celebrities, all dressed, jeweled, tuxedoed, and coiffured to the hilt. Then-President Ronald Reagan and Mrs. Reagan, former President Gerald Ford, Bob and Dolores Hope, Governor George Dukmejian, Dr. Armand Hammer, Herman Wouk, and many other notables from the worlds of entertainment, the arts, business, and politics were there. The Bob Hope Cultural Center, within which is the McCallum Theatre for the Performing Arts, is Coachella Valley's top venue for entertainment. It presents the world's leading performers and performing groups, such as Ella Fitzgerald, Leontyne Price, Kiri Te Kanawa, the Academy of St. Martin-in-the-Fields, the Alvin Ailey American Dance Theater, the London Symphony Orchestra, Tony Bennett, Roy Clark, and Reba McEntire.

Shopping

The resort communities of Greater Palm Springs have attractive shopping centers, specialty shops and boutiques, art galleries, and various services, such as banks and beauty and hairstyling salons. Within the valley you can purchase the latest fashions from France and Italy, the finest jewelry and furs, the best in golf and tennis equipment, expensive perfumes and leather accessories, and fine American Indian crafts. There are also countless bargain places where you can buy bathing suits, T-shirts, and all sorts of odds and ends. Some of the leading resorts, such as Marriott's Desert Springs, have extensive galleries of attractive shops on their premises.

DESERT FASHION PLAZA

Located in downtown Palm Springs, on North Palm Canyon Drive, this attractive complex contains such well-known retailing names as I. Magnin, Saks Fifth Avenue, Gucci, Laura Ashley, Brentano's Books, and the Sharper Image. High-fashion specialty shops include Champs-Elysées, Sabina Children's Fashions, Stuards for Men, and Isis. The plaza also has a number of dining places and services. Maxim's de Paris Suite Hotel is attached to the shopping mall.

Index

INDEX

196

INDEX

INDEX

INDEX

199

INDEX